THE PHILOSOPHY OF JESUS

Other titles of interest from St. Augustine's Press

Peter Kreeft, *The Sea Within: Waves and the Meaning of All Things*

Peter Kreeft, *Socratic Logic*

James V. Schall, *The Regensburg Lecture*

James V. Schall, *The Sum Total of Human Happiness*

St. Augustine, *On Order [De Ordine]*

St. Augustine, *The St. Augustine LifeGuide*

Thomas Aquinas, *Commentary on the Epistle to the Hebrews*

Thomas Aquinas, *Commentaries on St. Paul's Epistles to Timothy, Titus, and Philemon*

Thomas Aquinas, *Disputed Questions on Virtue*

John of St. Thomas, *Introduction to the Summa Theologiae of Thomas Aquinas*

C.S. Lewis, *The Latin Letters of C.S. Lewis*

Josef Pieper, *Leisure, the Basis of Culture*

Josef Pieper, *The Silence of St. Thomas*

Josef Pieper, *The Concept of Sin*

Joseph Bobik, *Veritas Divina: Aquinas on Divine Truth*

Gabriel Marcel, *The Mystery of Being*, in two volumes

John Paul II, *The John Paul II LifeGuide*

Dietrich von Hildebrand, *The Heart*

Dietrich von Hildebrand, *The Dietrich von Hildebrand LifeGuide*

Servais Pinckaers, O.P., *Morality: The Catholic View*

Peter Augustine Lawler, *Homeless and at Home in America*

Michael Davis, *Wonderlust: Ruminations on Liberal Education*

A. J. Conyers, *Last Things: The Heart of New Testament Eschatology*

Karl Rahner, S.J., *Encounters with Silence*

THE PHILOSOPHY OF JESUS

By Peter Kreeft

ST. AUGUSTINE'S PRESS
South Bend, Indiana
2007

Manufactured in the United States of America.

2 3 4 5 6   13 12 11 10 09 08 07

Library of Congress Cataloging in Publication Data
Kreeft, Peter.
The philosophy of Jesus / by Peter Kreeft.
p.   cm.
Includes index.
ISBN 1-58731-635-8 (hardcover: alk. paper)
1. Jesus Christ – Teachings. 2. Jesus Christ – Person and offices. 3. Christianity – Philosophy.
4. Catholic Church – Doctrines. I. Title.
BS2415.K695 2007
232.9'54 – dc22   2007000833

∞ *The paper used in this publication meets the minimum requirements of the American National Standard for Information Sciences – Permanence of Paper for Printed Materials, ANSI Z39.48-1984.*

St. Augustine's Press
www.staugustine.net

Contents

Introduction I: Who Is this Book For?

IT IS FOR BOTH Christians and non-Christians.

(1) It's designed to show Christians a new dimension of Jesus: Jesus the philosopher.

(2) And it's designed to show non-Christians a new dimension of philosophy, a new philosophy and a new philosopher. It's not designed to convert them.

But I am a Christian as well as a philosopher; that is, I believe Jesus is God. And I won't hide that or fake it. That's why I capitalize His name throughout the book.

But wait! If I just lost your potential readership by that statement, I challenge you—as a philosopher, now, not as a Christian—to ask yourself this question before you leave, and to give a logical answer: would you refuse to read a book about the philosophy of Buddha just because it was written by a Buddhist? Or a book explaining the philosophy of the Qur'an just because it was written by a

Muslim? Wouldn't it make more sense to refuse to read it if it *wasn't*?

Introduction II:
Why Is Jesus a Philosopher?

WHAT? JESUS, A PHILOSOPHER? Would He give a lecture at Harvard, or engage in a long Socratic dialog in Plato's Academy, or write a critique of Kant's *Critique of Pure Reason?*

Obviously not. And everyone knows that. That is "trivially true."

In another sense, Jesus *was* a philosopher, but this second sense is also trivial. Everyone has some "philosophy of life." Even Homer Simpson is a philosopher.

But Jesus was a philosopher in a meaningful middle sense, the sense in which Confucius, Buddha, Muhammad, Solomon, Marcus Aurelius, and Pascal were philosophers.

I quote C.S. Lewis as my authority to support this classification, in a letter to Dom Bede Griffeths (*Collected Letters of C.S. Lewis, volume II.* San Francisco: Harper/SF, 2004, p. 191):

I question your account of Our Lord, when you say "He is essentially a poet and not at all a philosopher." Surely the "type of mind" represented in the human nature of Christ (and in virtue of His humanity we may, I suppose, neither irreverently nor absurdly speak of it as a "type of mind") stands at just about the same distance from the poetic as from the philosopher. . . . After all, how full of argument, of repartee, even of irony, He is. The passage about the denarius ("whose image and superscription?"); the dilemma about John's baptism; the argument against the Sadducees from the words "I am the God of Jacob, etc.": the terrible, yet almost humorous, trap laid for his Pharisaic host ("Simon, I have something to say to you"); the repeated use of the *a fortiori* ("If . . . how much more"); and the appeals to our reason ("Why do not ye of yourselves judge what is right?")—surely in all these we recognize as the human and natural vehicle of the Word's incarnation a mental complexion in which a keen-eyed peasant *shrewdness* is just as noticeable as an imaginative quality—something in other words quite as close (on the natural level) to Socrates as to Aeschylus.

Even about the parables . . . the mode in which the fable represents its truth is intellectual rather than imaginative—like a philosopher's *illustration* rather than a poet's *simile*. The unjust judge, to the imagination, presents no likeness to God—carries into the story no divine flavour or colour (as the Father of the Prodigal Son, for instance, does). His likeness to God is purely for the intellect. It is a kind of proportion sum—A:B::C:D.

But this book is not so much about Jesus' philosophical *style* or method or "cast of mind" but about his philosophical *substance*, his philosophical *answers*, his *philosophy*.

Introduction III: What Are the Four Great Philosophical Questions?

THERE ARE FOUR PERENNIAL philosophical questions. "Philosophy" means "the love of wisdom," and wisdom, if we had it, would give us answers to at least these four great questions:

1. What is? What is real? Especially, what is most real?
2. How can we *know* what is real, and especially the most real?
3. Who are we, who want to know the real? "Know thyself."
4. What *should* we be, how should we live, to be more real?

They are the questions about being, truth, self, and goodness. The divisions of philosophy that explore these four questions are called by four technical names: metaphysics, epistemology, philosophical anthropology, and ethics.

1. First things first: everything is relative to metaphysics. The first thing every baby wants to know is: What's there? My son's first question was "Wot dat?" He kept shooting the question at everything, like a machine gun, until he got a catalog of answers, a universe.

   If we are wise, we never grow up.

2. But we do change. Around the beginning of adolescence we turn critical: we want to know not just the difference between cats and dogs but the difference between truth and falsehood. We want to know how we can know, how we can be sure. We become epistemologists.

   And since the most interesting question of metaphysics is about *ultimate* reality, the most interesting question of epistemology is about knowing ultimate reality: how can we finite fools know infinite wisdom? How can man know God? Or even that there is a God?

3. A little later, we also turn inward. We wonder who we really are once we stop playing with our masks on other people's stages. Why is it so hard to "know thyself"? Obviously,

what we are is human beings, but what is *that*? ("Wot dat?") Once we know the known, we want to know the knower.

4. Finally, when we realize that this self that knows is fundamentally different from everything else in the known universe because it alone *can fail* to be its true self, we then demand to discriminate not only between truth and falsehood but also between good and evil. We can be bad or good. Nothing else in the universe has that choice. Our selves, unlike acorns or stars, are not wholly given to us but made by our choices. Once we realize that, we ask how we can become our true selves, our real selves, our good selves. How can bad people become good people? And what *is* it to be a good person? ("Wot dat?")

The logical order of questions is this: we must first know something real before we can know how we know it; and we must first know who we are before we can know what is good for us. The order is also an order of increasing concreteness, increasing practicality, and increasing accessibility and interest to ordinary people. Ethics is based on metaphysics, it is logically posterior to meta-physics; but it is psychologically more compelling.

Philosophers have thought profoundly about these four questions for over two millennia. Why have they not found answers that are adequate, final, and universally acknowledged? Why is one of the best definitions of a philosopher "one who con-tradicts other philosophers"? H.L. Mencken said, "Philosophy consists largely of one philosopher arguing that all the others are jackasses. He usual-ly proves it."

The Christian answer: because the only ade-quate and final answer to all four great philosoph-ical questions is Christ. The most philosophical writer in the Bible, John, begins his Gospel by identifying Jesus with the *Logos* ("In the beginning was the *Logos*, and the *Logos* was with God and the *Logos* was God . . . and the *Logos* became flesh and dwelt among us.") What is the *Logos*? It is an incredibly rich Greek word. Here are some of its meanings: the *Logos* means the Word of God, the Revelation of God, the Speech of God, the Wisdom of God, the Mind of God, the Truth of God, the Reason of God, the Philosophy of God.

Jesus is God's philosophy.

I. Jesus' Metaphysics

1. Jesus' Jewish Metaphysics

THE FIRST FACT WE must know about Jesus to understand his metaphysics—in fact, the one fact that is the necessary historical key to understanding everything He says, and the fact that has been denied, forgotten, ignored, or downplayed by every heretic in history, in one way or other—is the fact that Jesus was a Jew.

He was not a Gnostic or a New Ager. He was not a Modernist or secular humanist. He was not a Marxist or socialist. He was not a Platonic philosopher. He was not a Brahmin pantheist. He was not an Aryan racist. He was not a social worker or a pop psychologist or a pagan myth or a magician. He was not a Democrat or a Republican; in fact, he was not an American. He was not a libertarian or a monarchist or an anarchist or a radical or a neoconservative. He was not a medieval or a modern man. He was a Jew.

What does this have to do with metaphysics? Everything. Jesus knew the crucial answer to the crucial question of metaphysics because He was a Jew. The ultimate truth of metaphysics, the nature of ultimate reality, reality at its most real, was not the unknowable mystery to the Jews that it was to all the pagan tribes, nations, and religions around them.

This was not because the Jews were smarter than anyone else. It was because Ultimate Reality, for reasons known only to Himself, had chosen to reveal Himself to them as to no one else. God had come out of hiding.

In fact, He had told them His name. And that name was "I AM."

"I" is the name of a Person, not a Force. God is "He," not "It."

Half a hemisphere away, in India, great sages had reached the realization that Ultimate Reality was one, and that it was infinite; but they did not know that its name was "I." On the contrary, most of them taught that the "I," or "ego" ("ego" is simply the Latin word for "I"), that is, our sense of unique, irreducible, distinct, individual personhood, was the ultimate *illusion* and the great obstacle to supreme enlightenment.

This is probably why the East never developed a morality or a politics of human rights as did the Jewish, then Christian, then Muslim, West. For the metaphysical basis for the idea of the rights of man is the idea (or rather, the revealed truth) of man as created in the image of God. The rights of the human "I," and the very reality of the human "I," are grounded in the divine "I." The West had both its "I's" open, while the East was closed to both.

In fact, no two religions could differ more radically in their metaphysics than Judaism and Hinduism. That which Hinduism claimed to be the ultimate illusion and the ultimate obstacle to wisdom and enlightenment was precisely that which Judaism claimed to be ultimate reality and supreme wisdom. If a Jew said to his rabbi, "I just discovered that I'm God," the rabbi would rend his clothes and cry, "Blasphemy! Insanity! Arrogance! Idiocy!" But if a Hindu said that to his guru, the guru would smile and say, "Congratulations. You finally found out. Welcome to the ranks of the enlightened."

Hinduism and Judaism had both risen above paganism by realizing that God was one and perfect. Hindus reached that point from the bottom up, Jews from the top down: Hindus got there by human mystical experience, Jews got there by divine revelation.

Hinduism and Judaism were the two purest religions of the ancient world. Both religions rose above paganism by knowing that God was all-knowing, and therefore could never be escaped, tricked, conned, or bribed like the gods of pagan-ism. But the Jewish reason for this belief was different from the Hindu reason. The Jewish reason was that God knew all because He had *created* the universe; the Hindu reason was that God was *dreaming* the universe.

The idea of creation, in the proper sense, is a uniquely Jewish idea. It is expressed by a uniquely Jewish word: *bara'*. It is a word that has no equivalent in any other ancient language. It is a verb that never has any subject besides God. Only God can create. For to create means to make out of nothing, not out of something. It means to make the very existence of something, not just its form, meaning, structure, order, or destiny. Creating is not just making new form in old matter; it is making the very existence of the matter.

Not once in history did this idea, the idea of a single God creating the very existence of everything else out of nothing at all, ever enter any human mind except that of the Jews and those who learned from them (mainly Christians and Muslims).

Alone among the many ancient gods, the Jewish God was always "He," never "She" (or "It" or "They" or the Hermaphrodite). For "She" symbolized something immanent, while "He" was transcendent. "She" was the Womb of all things, the cosmic Mother, but "He" was *other* than Mother Earth. He created the earth, and He came into it from without, as a man comes into a woman. He impregnated nonbeing with being, darkness with light, dead matter with life, history with miracles, minds with revelations, His chosen people with prophets, and souls with salvation. He was *transcendent*.

That is why only Judaism, of all ancient religions, had no goddesses and no priestesses. For priests are representatives and symbols of gods. Priests mediate not only Man to God but also God to Man. Women can represent Man to God as well as men can, for women are equally human, valuable, good, and pious. But women cannot represent this God to Man, for God is not our Mother but our Father. *Earth* is our Mother.

Jesus *always* called God "Father." And Jesus was anything but a male chauvinist. He liberated women more than anyone else in His time. But He was also a Jew. He believed that Judaism was the revelation of the true God. He believed that *God* had taught us how to speak of Him. He not only *believed* this, He *knew* it, for He was there! He was (and is) the eternal *Logos* or Mind or Reason or Word of God. He was the Mind that had *invented* Judaism—unless He was a liar and Judaism was a lie.

Hindu monotheism had made peace with polytheism. To this day, Hindus worship many gods as well as one. Brahman Himself (or Itself) is equally manifested in Vishnu, the immanent "creator" of life, and in Shiva, the destroyer, and in Kali, Shiva's thousand-armed consort—and in literally thousands of named gods and goddesses. But for the Jews there simply were no other gods. With one startlingly unecumenical sweep of God's pen, all the gods of all the religions of the world were crossed out.

History has not been kind to polytheism. In the West, all the other gods are dead. (How many temples of Diana or Mithras or Zeus are listed in your Yellow Pages?) And so are their worshippers.

(When was the last time you talked with a Caananite or a Moabite or a Hittite?) Four thousand years after Abraham, half the people in the world have learned from the Jews that (as the Muslims say) "there is no God but God." He is the One, the Creator. He is unique.

That is the first point of Jesus' metaphysics. It is not original. Every Jew knew it. Anyone who ignores, doubts, or waters down that historical fact cannot possibly understand Jesus' philosophy.

And here is a second unique Jewish belief: that the divine Will is perfectly good and righteous and holy and just. God is the only god you can't bribe. And since that is the character of Ultimate Reality—and since in order to be really real we must conform to the character of Ultimate Reality—therefore the meaning of life is to be holy, to be a saint. Morality flows from metaphysics because goodness flows from God. "You must be holy because I the Lord your God am holy." The connection is repeated like a liturgical formula in the Torah. Unlike the gods of the polytheists and unlike the god of the pantheists, God has no dark side. And that is why we shouldn't have a dark side either. The consequences of the Jewish metaphysics for ethics have been world-shaking. The whole world got a Jewish mother, a Jewish conscience, because the world got the Jewish Father.

This divine goodness is not just perfect, it is more than perfect. It spills out beyond itself like sunlight. It is *agape*, generosity, altruism, self-giving, self-sacrificial love. God seeks intimacy with Man, God seeks to marry Man. "Your creator shall become your Husband," says Isaiah (54:5). To that end, He makes covenants, to prepare for the fundamental covenant, marriage.

No pagan ever suspected the possibility of such intimacy, even with their finite, anthropomorphic gods: that is, the relationship scripture calls "faith," or fidelity. And therefore no pagan ever understood the deeper meaning and terror of "sin" either, for sin is the breaking of that relationship. Sin is to faith what infidelity is to marriage. Only one who knows the wonder of marriage can know the horror of infidelity.

That is why Jesus, the Jew, took sin much more seriously than any pagan possibly could, and why He paid the ultimate price—His own life—to save us from it.

From the viewpoint of the purely rational philosopher, the most surprising thing about the

Jewish concept of God is not that God is one, or perfect, or good, or even loving, but that God, the infinite being, has a *character*. He is not just "the Ground of Being" but a person with a personality. And that person and His personality can be known (*connaitre, kennen*) by the experience of prayer, moral effort, repentance, and faith as a lived marriage-like relationship with Him. Though He is infinite, "infinite" does not mean "without character." He is infinitely *holy*, infinitely *righteous*, infinitely *just*, infinitely *loving*, etc. He is not everything in general and nothing in particular. He discriminates between good and evil, and demands we do the same, both in thought and in life. He gives each of us the inner prophet of conscience for that purpose: to be morally narrow-minded, to be judgmental, to be discriminating between good and evil. For He is infinitely narrow-minded: He will not compromise with evil. And if we are to live in His family, as His children, we must do the same. Just as His only-begotten Son is just like His Daddy, we His adopted children must be just like Daddy too. That's why He says to us, "You must be perfect as My Father in Heaven is perfect." (Matthew 5:48)

Religious Jews before Jesus had already learned

from their own prophets most of these startling truths about God (though they did not know that God had an eternal Son), and thus about Ultimate Reality, and thus about metaphysics. All Jesus did was to *show* what they already *knew*, to show it "up close and personal," to put God's face "in their face." He did not show them a new God or teach a new concept of God or a new attribute of God, but He gave them a new *deed* of God, the greatest of all divine deeds, the Incarnation, and in it the redemption by His divine suffering, death, and resurrection.

The Father and the Son are the same God, for "he who has seen Me has seen the Father" (John 14:9). "Like father, like son." Jesus was not God represented but God presented, God made maximally present, God known by sight and even touch as well as by faith. Heaven had come to earth. It was not a new concept of Heaven but a new presence of Heaven. Jesus showed His chosen people thirty-three years of Heaven. For Heaven is where God is. God defines Heaven, Heaven does not define God.

2. Jesus' New Name for God

The name Jesus called God was an even more

startling one than the one God had revealed to Moses. Through Moses the Jews had learned that God is simply I AM, the one, eternal, perfect, unique, utterly real Person. Now Jesus called this Person a name no one had ever dreamed or dared to use: "Father."

That meant two shocks: God was Jesus' Father by nature in eternity and our Father by adoption in time.

("Adopted *son*" was the generic legal title for adopted females as well as males in the ancient world, since the right of inheritance passed through males. So "son" was the necessary word to designate the fact that women as well as men had the right of full spiritual inheritance of all God's riches through Christ. The really "inclusive" point could only be expressed through the apparently "exclusive" word.)

And Jesus went even further. His word was "Abba"—not just "Father" but "Daddy," the intimate term used by a child, or even a baby. (Even a baby can bubble "Abba" or "Dada.") The infinitely transcendent One was now and for the rest of time and eternity also the infinitely intimate One. The Father is now in Baby's playpen playing with Baby in baby-talk. The inaccessible Deity became so accessible that He could be murdered. He made accessible not just His spirit but His blood. His saving words of power were not, like a philosopher's, "This is my mind" but "This is My Body." (Matthew 26:26)

St. John the apostle is still stunned and astounded in his old age as he ponders this paradox when penning his first epistle. The first sentence of his Gospel said: "In the beginning was the Word, and the Word was with God and the Word was God . . . and the Word was made flesh and dwelt among us, and we saw His glory." The first sentence of his epistle said: "That-which-was-from-the-beginning [became] that-which-we-have-looked-upon-and-touched-with-our-hands." The unmanifest Source of all manifestations became manifested. The "Tao" beyond and behind "the ten thousand things under heaven" became one of those things.

The equation of God with Christ is like the equation of E with MC squared. The divine energy was converted into matter, in a kind of trans-nuclear fission. The divine subject ("I") became a human object ("him"). The speed of Heavenly light became finite.

Why did He do it?

3. The Metaphysics of Love

"So that you may have fellowship with us, and our fellowship is with the Father and with His Son Jesus Christ." (I John 1:3) The "bottom line" or practical payoff of the theological paradox of the Incarnation is the religious opportunity of fellowship, or intimacy, with Ultimate Reality. This is the most radical solution to the fundamental problem of metaphysics: how to know Being. Being ("AM") turned out to be also Person ("I"), and knowing turned out to be marrying! The object of metaphysics proposes to the metaphysician. It is as utterly unexpected as if when Newton discovered gravity he had heard a voice coming from all the gravity in the universe: "Will you marry me?" It is as if the square of the hypotenuse had confessed it was in love with Pythagoras.

Only love could motivate such madness. Christ's outstretched arms on the Cross are God's answer to our childlike question: "How much do you love me?" "This much!" How big is that stretch? It is the distance between Heaven and earth that was bridged by the Incarnation, and it was the distance between Heaven and Hell that was bridged by our salvation.

Christ is the ultimate revelation of God, or

ultimate reality, of the deepest secret of metaphysics. Man's metaphysical quest finds its final earthly fulfillment at Golgotha, the Place of the Skull, where the world saw the most dramatic event in history: Death and Life dueling in miraculous combat (*Mors et Vita duello, conflixere mirando,* in the words of the "Dies Irae"). Life conquered Death not by power but by love. The Little Lamb defeated the Great Beast by using His secret weapon: His blood, His love. He let the Beast drink His blood, like a reverse Dracula.

He could have redeemed us with one drop of blood; why did He die such a bloody death? Because He had more blood to give. To the scandal of the scholars, God's answer to our metaphysical quest is not a concept or a mythic symbol but that deed. You can *see* the nature of ultimate reality when you look at a crucifix. There is more metaphysical wisdom in that simple gaze of the simple Christian child than in the highest mystical experiences of the sage or guru, and more than in the finest philosophical systems of a Plato or an Aristotle. They may have known the experience of Being or the concept of Being, but the Christian child sees Being's face.

How could any mortal man have dared to

imagine such a story? How could the human heart have ever conceived such a thought? The effect cannot exceed the cause. Such a thought—that the perfect God should act as if He stood in desperate need of us sinners—is far too absurd to be anything but either Hellish insanity or Heavenly revelation.

How else, but for Christ, could we have known that God loves us? I mean *really* loves us, not just with proper philanthropy but with utterly improper passion. Even if any man dared to hope this, what ground could there possibly be for such a crazy hope? What data do we have? What evidence? Certainly not nature ("nature red in tooth and claw"), or human life ("solitary, poor, nasty, brutish, and short"), or human history ("the slaughter-bench at which the happiness of peoples is sacrificed"). The only data we have to know that God is love is Christ.

Yet once revealed, the absurd story appears totally beautiful. Tolkien says of the Gospel, "There is no tale men more wish to be true." For life's greatest joy is to be loved, passionately loved, infinitely loved; to be totally known, with all our wrinkles, and yet totally loved.

Sartre, in *No Exit*, shows how apparently

impossible this is: for me to know you is for me to know all the things that make you not lovable, he argues, and for me to love you is for me to love an ideal, a dream, a fantasy of my own. Only God made the impossible possible. To be loved and known at once: that is Heavenly. Remember the joy you felt when you received even a little of that, even the tiniest approximation to that, from one little stupid, sinful human being like yourself? Now multiply that by infinity, which is the difference between humanity and divinity, and you begin to understand the joy of being known and loved by God. Loved how much? *This* much. Christ-much.

But we live in the shadow of sinfulness, the light-absorbing clothing that we wear over the divine glory we were created with, and that is why the love of God seems less piercing and powerful to us than the love of a man or a woman. But that shadow was lifted by Christ. That was the veil that hid the Holy of Holies in the Temple, and He tore it. In Heaven, when with purified eyes we can endure the sight, the veil will be lifted totally. As of now, we can endure only an inch of light from the empty tomb. (Remember that last scene in Mel Gibson's *The Passion of the Christ*?) Perhaps that is why Christ did not allow us to be actual eyewitnesses of the event of His resurrection: it would have blinded us.

4. The Moral Consequences of Metaphysics

The consequences of this metaphysics for morality are momentous. Since love "goes all the way up" into Ultimate Reality, into God, so does morality. Real morality (as distinct from legalistic or pragmatic or political morality) is grounded in metaphysics. For the essence of morality, *agape* love, is the essence of Divine Being. Christ revolutionized metaphysics by revealing not just love but the metaphysics of love, the fact that love is the essence of God; that love is, in the absolutely last analysis, "the way it is."

All explanation is a relationship between A and B: A is explained by B, and B by C, and C by D. But eventually there has to be something that is not explained by anything else, but just by itself. Of that something we must simply say, "because that's just the way it is." Christ revealed that "the way it is" is love. The ultimate equation is not "Being is Being" but "God is love." (I John 4:8)

It is this ultimate truth about "the way it is," the truth that God is love, that is the reason behind the other astonishing paradox of Christianity, that the absolutely one God is a Trinity of Persons. The reason is that the supremely single thing, the supreme oneness, is the oneness of love, not of number or of matter. Matter follows the laws of matter, which are the laws of mathematics, the laws of quantity. Matter is that which can be quantified. But mathematical, arithmetical unity is not the highest kind of unity, the most unified kind of unity. Rather, the active, personal identification of the lover's identity with the beloved's identity is the higher unity. And by "higher" unity here I mean not just "better" but also "more truly *one.*"

We can see faint but definite indications of this even in our faint loves, if only they are definite. The lover finds his unity, his identity, his self, his "I," more in his beloved than in himself.* The death or suffering or sin of the beloved is far more of a threat to the lover's own life and identity and joy than his own could ever be. We know this strange fact by experience only if we are lovers. Thus we know by experience the basis for the Trinity. We know it not by theorizing but only by practicing love, by practicing what the Trinity is.

But the theory can then follow, like a shadow,

---

* Were I a woman, I would say "her" unity and "herself." I will not say "his or her self" or "themselves" because abusing grammar is not reparation for the sin of abusing grandmas.

if the lived substance comes first. And the theory is this: that love, which we have already seen to be the highest and most unified kind of unity, requires more than one person, unless it is merely selfish love, auto-eroticism. It requires a lover and a beloved, an other.

And the love between the lover and the beloved at the highest level can be so real that it is a reality in itself, a third person. For love is fruitful and creative. Human sexuality is a pale but holy image of that ultimate fact. *That* is why the fleeting act of human sex is so ecstatic in both senses of that word: unutterably joyful and mystically standing-outside-oneself. It surpasses anything possible on a merely animal level because it is an image of the infinite and eternal ecstasy of the Trinity.

If God were only one Person, only a Lov*er*, instead of complete Love, He would *need* an other to love, and thus God would be in need of His creatures. Or else, He would *not* need any other, and then His love would be only love-of-self. Even when such "selfish" love is not competitive and sinful, it cannot produce the ecstasy and the joy that unselfish love can and does produce, both spiritually and sexually.

Since God is complete, He is complete love: Lover, Beloved, and Loving all in one: subject of love, object of love, and act of love. Each of these three is so real in God that they are not just mentally-distinguished, abstract aspects but really-distinct, concretely real Persons.

So the nature of ultimate reality is Trinity: not only absolute oneness but also absolute manyness. Plurality as well as unity "goes all the way up." This too is revealed only by Christ. No one who does not believe in Christ believes in the Trinity. The data for the ultimate secret of metaphysics is Christ. Christ is the world's greatest metaphysician.

5. Sanctity as the Key to Ontology

And because saints are "little Christs," Gabriel Marcel is right when he says that "sanctity is the true introduction to ontology." ("On the Ontological Mystery," in *The Philosophy of Existentialism.*)

That is one of the most puzzling and pregnant sayings I have ever heard from any philosopher. It is not sentimentalism; it is perfect logic. For:

(1) Ontology, or metaphysics, is the science of being.

(2) And our clearest understanding of being, or reality, must come from the most real being, not from the less real.

(3) And the most real being, the source and standard and archetype of all reality, is God.

(4) But we don't know God directly, as an object, for His name is not "IT IS" (object) but "I AM" (subject).

(5) And we too are subjects ("I's"), not objects, since we are created in His image.

(6) Yet we can and do know ourselves somehow.

(7) So it is personhood, or I-ness, that is the key, or door, or window, to metaphysics.

(8) But personhood, like being, is analogical. It is a matter of degree. We are more or less authentic, more or less real. Atoms are not as real as souls, and human souls are not as real as God.

(9) The most real human persons are saints. They are what we are all designed to be.

(10) Therefore the study of sanctity is the key to the study of being.

Let's go through that again, this time emphasizing the central role of Christ.

(1) Metaphysics is the science of being.

(2) The nature of being is the nature of God, for all being is defined by God, the Creator of all

being. For instance, all being is good because God is good and all being is either the Creator, who is supremely good, or a creature created by the Creator, and therefore also good.

(3) God "speaks" or "expresses" or "reveals" Himself in His *Logos*, His eternal Word, His Mind. This is the eternal Christ. Jesus is His human name, *Logos* is His eternal name; it is the same Person. God the Father holds nothing back in expressing His whole self in God the Son.

(3) God the Son became a man, and gave us the final, definitive, perfect revelation of God, and therefore of Being.

(4) Saints are little Christs. We see Christ through the saints. Saints are windows who let through more of the light of Christ, which is the light of the Father, which is the light of Being.

(5) That is why saints are the windows to being, and why the study of sanctity is the key to metaphysics.

Marcel's saying refutes our foolish and harmful habit of separating metaphysics and sanctity into very separate compartments. On the one hand, metaphysics is supposed to be objective and impersonal. But the ultimate object of metaphysics, the ultimate being, ultimate reality, is a Person. His name is "I AM." On the other hand, sanctity is supposed to be subjective and psychological. But the ultimate point of being a saint is to be real, to be Godlike, to conform to and thus reveal the ultimate nature of objective reality.

Another way to see the connection between metaphysics and sanctity is by remembering two of the names of God, the one God: God is love (*agape*) and God is also Necessary Being, the Unchangeable Way Things Are, the Utterly Real, Ultimate Reality. So ultimate reality is *agape* love. So the object of metaphysics is the object of sanctity.

Still another formulation: To succeed at metaphysics we must know the utterly real; to know the utterly real we must love; to love is to be a saint; therefore to succeed at metaphysics is to be a saint.

6. The Metaphysics of "I AM"

Until the Incarnation, the Jews were forbidden to have any image or picture of God. For God's essence, revealed in the name He gave to Moses in the burning bush (Exodus 3:14), was "I AM." God is pure subject, not object. There is no picture of God because God is the one behind the camera.

Back when cameras were new, Grandpa was the only one in the family who took all the family pictures. So the rest of the family always appeared in his pictures, but he did not. He had the only camera, and it was up to him to give the camera to another family member so he could pose for a picture of himself. This is what God did in the Incarnation. Being became *a* being, the Subject became an object, God became a man, I AM became a He.

But He is still I AM. Watch how He interacts with His creatures now, and you will detect the metaphysical secret in the name "I AM."

> "Your father Abraham rejoiced that he was to see my day; he saw it and was glad."
>
> The Jews then said to him, "You are not yet fifty years old; have you seen Abraham?"
>
> Jesus said to them, "Truly, truly I say to you, before Abraham was, I AM."
>
> So they took up stones to throw at him. (John 8:57–58)

One of the most striking pieces of evidence about who Jesus is—I AM, the Subject, not the object—is how He always manifests this identity in His interactions with His creatures. In all His encounters, He becomes in time what He is eternally. He is the First, and so He cannot be the second. He is the Subject, and so He cannot be the object.

He cannot be the object of human manipulation and control unless He consents to be. This consent culminates, of course, in His crucifixion. But remember that He had said, "I lay down My own life. No man takes it from Me." (John 10:18)

Nor can He be the object of human understanding and comprehension. For "the light shines in the darkness and the darkness was not able to comprehend it." (John 1:5) When He is questioned by His enemies, when they try to put Him on the spot and pin Him down to their walls, when they try to make Him the object of their control and of their comprehension, He not only escapes, but He reverses the relationship so that He becomes the questioner and they become the questioned ones. (Jesus perfectly understands the archetypal Jewish joke: Tell me, why does a rabbi always answer a question with another question? Answer: Why shouldn't a rabbi answer a question with another question?)

(1) "Shall we stone the adulteress or not?"

(If so, you defy Rome. If not, you defy Moses.)

"Let him who is without sin cast the first stone." (John 8:7)

(2) "Should we pay taxes to Caesar or not?"

(Is Caesar your king or not? These were the very men who would soon shout, 'We have no king but Caesar!')

"Render to Caesar what is Caesar's and to God what is God's" (instead of vice versa, which is what they were doing). (Luke 20:25)

(3) "By whose authority do you do these miracles?"

"By whose authority did John the Baptist preach to you repentance?"

"We cannot tell."

"Then I will not tell you by whose authority I do these miracles." (Matthew 21:27)

(4) "You shall love the Lord your God with your whole heart, and your neighbor as yourself, but who is my neighbor?"

And, after telling the parable of the Good Samaritan, "Go and do likewise." (Answer the question about who is the neighbor by *being* the neighbor—as I am doing.) (Luke 10:37)

(5) "Lord, are many saved?"

"Strive to enter in." (Luke 13:24)

What is common to all these examples is that the judge and the judged change places. Christ the Tiger bursts the bars of the cage men try to put around Him, and captures His would-be captors inside. He is the Fisherman, the Fisher-King, and we are the fish, not vice versa. This Fisherman cannot be caught like a fish. He fits into no net and swallows no bait, not even the Devil's temptations in the wilderness. There is no place in His mouth for a hook to hold, for His mouth is fire.

This phenomenon is especially clear in John's Gospel. It begins early, with the very first words John records as coming from His lips: "What do you seek?" (John 1:38) The question may seem casual and common, but it is profound.

It is profound because it is a probe that goes into the depths of our heart. It means, "What do you love the most?" And this means, "Who are you?" For we are what we love. We become what we love. We "identify with" what we love. We find our *identity* in what we love. St. Augustine knew that well; that's why he wrote: *Amor meus, pondus meum* – "my love is my gravity," my weight, my destiny. We become what we love the most, what we send out hearts out to. Our heredity makes us *what* we are, but our hearts make us *who* we are.

Jesus says the same thing: "Ask, and it shall be given to you. Seek, and you shall find. Knock, and the door will be opened to you. For all who ask, will receive, all who seek, will find, all who knock, will have the door opened." (Matthew 7:7) In other words, what you love, you will get. So be careful what you love.

So this is a very dangerous thing, this loving-thing. It changes you. It changes your life. It's as objectively real as a large, hot rock thrown in your face. It's not just a thought or a feeling inside you; it really happens. We unite with what we love. We become what we love. The more you love choco-late, the more chocolate you become. The more you love cannibalism, the more cannibalistic you become. The more you love Christ, the more Christlike you become. Nothing is more scary than that. Look how scared the world was of Christ: they had to crucify Him.

Do you want that? Jesus asks you, "What do you want?" just as personally and just as insistently as He asked His first disciples. We think we are on a quest for Him, but He questions our quest, He questions our heart. He is on a quest for us. He is the questioner, and we must answer Him, not vice versa. This is exactly what Job discovered when he met God. It is also what Viktor Frankl observed some of the prisoners in Auschwitz discovering: that this outrage that had happened to them, this suffering that was too big to get their minds around, this terrible thing that they were questioning as to its meaning ("Why must I suffer so?")—that this was not the answer but the question; that they could find the answer to their question only through their own action; that they were the answer and life was the question rather than vice versa. And this was true whether they believed that there was a God who stood behind "life," wearing it as His mask, or whether it was just "life" asking them the question.

In these four little words, "What do you want?" Jesus is asking not just one question but many. He is asking, for instance, the question that most of the Jews of His time were answering wrongly, just as most Gentiles do today: Do you want a political Messiah? A means to your political ends, whatever they may be, Left or Right, socialist or libertarian, Monarchist or Marxist, Herodian or Zealot, collaborationist or rebel? In His question He was giving an answer to their question ("Are you our Messiah?"). He was saying: "If you want a supernatural means to your natural end, I am *not* your Messiah. Do not come to Me." (That was probably why Judas betrayed Him.

Politics has been betraying religion ever since, from the Inquisition to Al Queda.)

In these four words He was also addressing a smaller group, the apolitical ecclesiastics who saw Him as a rabbi rather than as a rebel, and He was asking them: "Do you want a teacher who will pat and pander and patronize you and reinforce your self-esteem and self-satisfied, respectable pride? A contrast to that troublemaker John the Baptist? Someone who will condemn and upset your enemies the Romans but not you? If so, then do not come to Me. I am not your Messiah."

And He was also addressing an even smaller but significant group of people, His scholarly and philosophical contemporaries, and their followers down through the centuries, and He was asking them: "Do you want a rational philosopher who will not surprise or confuse you? The kind of teacher who will make you secure by telling you what you already know rather than insecure by challenging you to go beyond the safe little beach of human knowledge, even the profoundest human knowledge, out into the deep with the terrifying waves, where you actually *meet* the All-Holy One in whose presence you will "fall down at His feet as one dead?" (Revelation 1:7) Do you want to meet satisfyingly intelligent ideas rather than God? Or, if you do meet God, do you want to meet Him as an uncle rather than as an earthquake (to use Rabbi Abraham Heschel's memorable words)? If that's what you want, do not come to Me. I am not your Messiah."

Our fundamental question to Jesus—"Who are you?"—rebounds off him and hits us full in the face. He does not answer our question, "Who are you?" until we first answer His question, "Who are *you*? What do you want?" We come to Him hoping He is the answer to our question, and we find Him asking us whether we are the question to His answer.

This is not a trick, like a riddle, or even an optional, chosen method, like the Socratic Method. It is an ontological inevitability, because of Who He is. He is God. God is not our Answer Man, our servant, the means to our end. To think that is pagan anthropomorphism. No, God *is* the End. He is the Absolute; He is not relative to us, but we to Him. He is the First, the Creator, the Initiator. He is the Wooer, and we the wooed; He is the Impregnator, and we are the impregnated; He is the Bridegroom; we are the bride. (The image of the wooing may be socially relative, but the image of the impregnation is not. That is why God is always "He" and never "She" in the Bible. To think the reverse is to commit a metaphysical mistake, a solecism against the grammar of being, a sin of the mind against the unchangeable nature of ultimate reality.)

This is the God of Abraham, the real God. Abraham's Muslim children have never succumbed to the temptation of pop psychology, relativism, subjectivism, secular humanism, or "politically correct" feminism, as many American Jews and Christians have. (They have different temptations, like Islamo-fascism. None of us is immune.)

All the encounters between Christ and us in the four Gospels are structured by the fact that God is the great I AM; the subject, not the object; the questioner, not the answerer; the judge, not the judged; the initiator, not the responder. That is one of the clues, one of the fingerprints, so to speak, of the true God; and when pious Jews or Muslims read the Gospels, it is possible for them to find this clue based on their own scriptures. Christ speaks of this possibility when He says, "Everyone who has heard and learned from the Father comes to Me." (John 6:45) and "If you believed Moses, you would believe Me." (John 5:46)

This possibility, or clue—the clue to Christ's divinity to be found in the fact that He is always the initiator, not the responder—is exactly what we should expect if only two premises are true. The first is the essence of Christianity: that Christ is the Son of God. The second is that the principle "like father, like son" is true not only literally and biologically but also analogically and theologically, since biological reality is derived from theological reality as the creature is derived from the Creator. What follows is that to truly know either one, Father or Son, is to know the other.

Imagine a pious Muslim. A pious Muslim is simply one who is filled with true "islam," or submission and surrender to the one God, whom Muslims call "Allah" ("Allah" means, simply and literally, "the one God"). The Muslim has deep reverence for his prophet Muhammad precisely because he sees in him the perfect example of "islam" to Allah. When Allah commands, Muhammad obeys. When Allah says "recite!", Muhammad recites.

Now imagine this Muslim reading the Gospels for the first time. He would be impressed by the fact that Jesus, like Muhammad, is totally obedient to the Father. ("I came into the world not to do my own will but the will of my Father." . . . "My teach-ing is not my own, but my Father's.") This fact would reinforce the Muslim's belief that Jesus is a great prophet. But then comes a puzzle: unlike Muhammad, Jesus is always the judge, never the one judged. The Qur'an itself labels Muhammad a sinner, whom Allah commands to repent of his sins. But Jesus says, "Which of you can convict me of sin?" And what would this Muslim make of the fact that after railing against the blasphemously "unfitting" Christian notion that Allah should have a son, Muhammad suddenly and surprisingly declares, "But know that if Allah did have a Son, I would be the first to worship him"?

Is there the faintest note of uncertainty there, like David's in Psalm 139:19–24?

The divine fingerprint that the Muslim might detect in Jesus' words in the Gospels is not merely the fact that He claims divinity. Madmen have done that too, and Muslims claim that the mad-men here were the Christians who wrote the Gospels, not Christ. The divine fingerprint I speak of is the *style* of His claims. Whenever He is asked a question, He turns the situation around so that the questioner is questioned. Whenever He is asked an abstract, impersonal question, He gives a concrete, personal answer. When He is asked who He claims to be, He gives them not an objectifiable name, like "Zeus," but the holy, unique Name of His Father that declares His real presence: "I AM!"

Imagine the greatest philosophers in the world holding a conference on the existence of God: atheists versus theists. After all the arguments for atheism, the case for theism is presented by a visitor: God Himself, Who shows up at the conference not as a philosopher defending a theory but as *data,* creeping up behind the philosophers and saying, "BOO!"

That is the high and holy joke of Aquinas in the most famous of all his articles, the one on the existence of God in the *Summa.* (Aquinas has the same kind of sense of humor Jesus has: it is at the opposite extreme from jokes: it is an irony that resides deep in the very substance of what he is talking about.) In each article in the *Summa,* Aquinas, after listing objections to his thesis, defends it in two steps: first, in the section that begins with the formula "on the contrary," with an authoritative quotation, and then, in the section that begins with the formula "I answer that," with an original argument. So what authoritative quotation about God's existence does Aquinas use? Not any quote about God but a quote *from* God: "On the contrary, it is said in the person of God Himself, 'I AM.'" God sneaks into the conference debate and presents Himself as evidence. It is like a teenager's "Hel—*loooo!*" to her parents when they're talking about her in her presence as if she were not there. This is the humor Jesus Himself used in John 8:58. The response He got was rocks thrown at Him. It is also the same humor Socrates used in the *Apology* when, on trial for atheism, he brought into court as his character witness the word of a *god*, from the Delphic oracle. The response Socrates got was hemlock. People don't like to be subtly and gently laughed at by their own innocent victims.

This situation endures to the end of time, since Jesus endures to the end of time, and He is "the same yesterday, today, and forever." (Hebrews 13:8) The Incarnation had a beginning but not an ending. It forever divided time in two, cutting the Gordian knot of history. Abraham looked forward to the beginning of this event, while we look backward to it, but God looks neither forward nor backward, since He is not merely a character in His own play but the Playwright. For God it is a timeless truth that human flesh and blood, body and soul, is joined to His Son, the Divine Word of God, in hypostatic union. As the Athanasian Creed says, the Incarnation happened not by the lowering of divinity into humanity, as if divinity could suffer change, but by the raising of humanity into divinity. *We* suffer change, *we* are potentially this or that, but God is purely actual. We are potentially divinizeable, but God is not *potentially* humanizeable. God is purely actual. (That is the first meaning of "act.") Therefore He acts (that is the second meaning of "act"), while we are also acted upon. The divine nature cannot be acted upon. It cannot be changed. It is not passive or potential. Only when He assumes human nature can He be acted upon by us. And then He is acted upon even to the point of our scorns, our thorns, and our nails.

In the Incarnation, "I AM" became "HE WAS conceived of the Holy Spirit and born of the Virgin Mary." Then, on Calvary, the *I* who became a *he* became an *it:* the God who became a man became a corpse.

But then there was (or rather *is*) "the rest of the story": the Resurrection. The startling point for metaphysics is that this whole story is the *story* of *Being*.

II. Jesus' Epistemology

THE FIRST GREAT PHILOSOPHICAL question is: What is? The second, which naturally follows, is: How do we know what is? The first question is about being, the second is about truth.

Truth is relative to being, for "truth" means "the truth about being." "An orange is round" is *true* only because an orange *is* round.

Jesus' answer to the first question, the question of being, was Himself. It was not to point but to be, to be "I AM." So His answer to the second question, the question of truth, is also not to point to anything else as the truth but simply to *be* Himself the truth: "I AM the truth." (John 14:6)

Thus the supreme irony of Pilate cynically addressing the philosophers' great question "What is truth?" to the eternal, perfect, absolute, divine, eternal truth Himself, made incarnate and concrete and personal and standing before him, condemned. Pilate's skepticism implicitly complains:

"How am I supposed to know that great philosophical will-o-the-wisp, 'truth'? Can I see it? Can I touch it?" And Jesus answers: "Yes. In fact, you can crucify it."

But when man crucifies truth, truth crucifies man. In the very act whereby Pilate condemns truth incarnate, truth unincarnate condemns Pilate.

Jesus does not answer Pilate in words because truth incarnate is like light, not like a lit object. Jesus is not on trial, Pilate is. When we juxtapose Jesus with this second great philosophical question, the epistemological question, we see the same pattern repeated as we saw with the first question: just as Jesus is not a metaphysician but something more metaphysical than a metaphysician—He is the very being that all metaphysics seeks—so he is not just an epistemologist but the truth that all epistemology seeks. For Jesus is not a philosopher, a lover of wisdom, only because He *is* wisdom. He is the Beloved that "the love of wisdom" is in love with. The title of this book is appropriate because Jesus is more philosophical than any philosopher, not less.

He is the answer to Job's great, perennial quest:

Surely there is a mine for silver
And a place for gold which they refine.

Iron is taken out of the earth
And copper is smelted from the ore.
Men put an end to darkness
And search out to the farthest bound the ore in
    deep darkness.
The open shafts in a valley away from where men
    live;
They are forgotten by travelers,
They hang afar from men, they swing to and fro . . .
Man puts his hand to the flinty rock
And overturns mountains by the roots.
He cuts out channels in the rocks
And his eye sees every precious thing.
He binds up streams so that they do not trickle,
And the thing that is hid he brings forth to light.

But where shall wisdom be found?
And where is the place of understanding?
Man does not know the way to it
And it is not found in the land of the living.
The deep says: "It is not in me."
And the sea says: "It is not with me."
It cannot be gotten for gold
And silver cannot be weighed as its price.
Whence then comes wisdom?
And where is the place of understanding?
It is hid from the eyes of all the living
And concealed from the birds of the air . . .

God understands the way to it
And he knows its place. (Job 28)

What place is that? Jesus. Jesus is the place of wisdom. Jesus alone reveals both God and man to man, because He alone is perfect God and He alone is perfect man. As Pascal says,

> Not only do we only know God through Jesus Christ, but we only know ourselves through Jesus Christ; we only know life and death through Jesus Christ. Apart from Jesus Christ we cannot know the meaning of our life or our death, of God or of ourselves. (*Pensées* 417)

What must we know? Only two things: who we are and who God is. For these are the only two persons we will never be able to escape from, to all eternity. And knowing who we are involves knowing what the meaning of our life is, and that involves knowing the meaning of death, for death defines life as a frame defines a picture. Pascal's claim (which is the claim of Jesus Himself, and of all His disciples who wrote the New Testament) is that He is the answer, the true and final and ultimate and only adequate answer, to all four of Pascal's questions: God, self, life, and death.

Of these four questions, the first is God. God is the first question because God is the first in every way. We must begin with the Beginning. The most necessary thing to know is the most Necessary Being.

But this is impossible, for "He dwells in inaccessible light." (third canon of the Mass) How can the Eternal Subject, I AM, become the object of human knowledge? How can mere mortal man, how can this finite, fallen, fallible fool, know God? Far easier for a mentally retarded amoeba to know man.

Christ's answer comes in two parts: first the bad news, then the good news.

The bad news (which we knew already if we were as wise as Job) is that we can't. "No man has seen God at any time." (John 1:18) Then, immediately, He gives us the good news: "The only-begotten Son, who is in the bosom of the Father, He has made Him known." (John 1:18) Man's universal search for God is a universal failure, like the Tower of Babel. Philosophy is ultimately the classic Vermont farmer joke: "Ya can't get there from here." But God's search for man is a success, and the name of that success is Jesus.

We can't know God, ultimate Truth, by climbing any human tower, whether it is built of the babble of words or of bricks. We can know God only if God climbs down, if He lets down Jacob's ladder from Heaven. Jesus is Jacob's ladder (He Himself says so: compare John 1:51 with Genesis 28:12), and the way we see this ladder is upside down: it really rests on Heaven, not on earth like the Tower of Babel. Its foundations cannot collapse like Babel's because they are not human thought and words (*logoi*) but the divine thought and Word (the *Logos:* John 1:1).

It is utterly reasonable that human reason cannot find God. To prove this, we need a basic principle of epistemology, which we will discover by looking at the various levels of human knowledge. For the levels of knowledge correspond to levels of reality, since knowledge corresponds to reality. (In fact "knowledge" *means* "correspondence to reality.")

Let us begin by supposing that you want to know something very inferior to yourself: some man-made abstraction, some idea or rule or number. In that case, all the activity comes from you. For an abstract idea can do nothing of itself. Its whole life comes from yours.

Next, suppose you want to know something that is inferior to yourself that is independently real but not alive, like a rock. It has a reality independent of your mind, but all the activity (except its very act existing and its nature) comes from you. You must go to it and study it. It does nothing but sit there passively and let itself be studied.

Next, suppose you want to know something alive, a plant. It has some activity of its own. It can change from seed to tree, from living to dead, from healthy to diseased. So it is a little harder to know, especially to predict. It is alive, and we speak of "the *mystery* of life." We do not speak of "the mystery of rocks." But it is still fairly easy to know, and mainly passive.

Next, suppose you want to know an animal. This is harder still because the animal has a much richer, higher level of reality. It is active. It can run away from you and hide from you, unlike a plant. You have to win its confidence. There is a mental life shared between you. But still, you are the initiator. We do not see guinea pigs doing laboratory experiments on men.

Now when you move up one more step, when the being you want to know is another human being, an equal, the activity is divided equally, or almost equally. (You do most of the activity in dialoging with babies, while the older, wiser person does most of the activity in dialoging with you.

That is why most of our prayer time should be spent in listening.)

Next, suppose you want to know an angel. If the angel does not reveal himself, you will know very little, almost nothing.

Finally, suppose you want to know God. Here *all* the activity must originate from Him. If He does not take the initiative, we simply cannot know Him.

This is why there must be divine revelation if there is to be knowledge of God.

But there is divine revelation, God did reveal Himself, and in many ways: first of all, by creating the universe, but last and most of all by Christ, the final, definitive revelation of God. There will be no more definitive revelation, until the end of time. "For in him all the fullness of God was pleased to dwell." (Colossians 1:19) This verse tells us that Christ is all of God that we can ever know because He is all of God that there is. There is no more in God than in Christ. The Father holds nothing back in the Son. Christ is the ultimate epistemological revelation of ultimate metaphysical reality. Christ is the key to epistemology.

Watch how this unfolds in the Gospels. Watch how He works, how He does much more than simply know the truth and teach it. Watch how He *is* the truth, not just as 2 plus 2 are 4 in an equation but as bees do *be* in a beehive. (Bee-ing is what bees *do*. Existing is an act.) Watch how epistemology comes alive because truth is alive and active and therefore able to free us. Watch how "the truth shall make you free":

> The scribes and Pharisees brought a woman who had been caught in adultery, and placing her in the midst they said to him, "Teacher, this woman has been caught in the act of adultery. Now in the law Moses commanded us to stone such. What do you say about her?" This they said to test him, that they might have some charge to bring against him. Jesus bent down and wrote with his finger on the ground. And as they continued to ask him, he stood up and said to them, "Let him who is without sin be the first to throw a stone at her." And once more he bent down and wrote with his finger on the ground. But when they heard it, they went away, one by one, beginning with the eldest, and Jesus was left alone with the woman standing before him. Jesus looked up and said to her,
>
> "Woman, where are they? Has no one condemned you?" She said, "No man, Lord."

And he said, "Neither do I condemn you;
go, and do not sin again." (John 8:3–11)

The scribes and Pharisees demand an answer
from Jesus to a question they are certain must trap
Him: what does He say should be done to this
woman who has been caught in the act of adultery?
The Law of Moses, i.e. the law of God, commanded them to stone her. (Note that the law did not
merely *allow* or *recommend* this punishment but
commanded it.) But Roman law forbade the Jews to
exercise the right of capital punishment for any
crime at all. (Note that this law did not merely *dis-
courage* but *forbade* this punishment to be meted
out by the Jews rather than by the Romans.) So if
Jesus says, "No, do not stone her," he disobeys
Moses, and is a heretic. If he says, "Yes, stone her,"
he disobeys Rome, and is a traitor. And if he says
neither, he disobeys the law of honesty and is a
coward.

No human wisdom could have escaped this
perfect trap. Only three answers are logically possible (yes, no, and nothing), and all three leave
Jesus condemned: by Mosaic law if he says no, by
Roman law if he says yes, and by the natural law if
he says neither.

Ah, but remember who He is. He is I AM. He

is the one who spoke to Moses from the burning bush when Moses tried to pin Him down by demanding His name. Then, it was He who pinned Moses down by giving him as His name the name no pious Jew would henceforth ever dare to pronounce. For to pronounce "I AM" is to claim to bear that name, to *be* that "I." "I" can only be said in the first person. Any other name can be said in the second person, the person addressed ("you") or in the third person, the person expressed or referred to ("him" or "her").

Now, 1500 years later, Jesus enacts the same role reversal He enacted at the burning bush, by making His answer a question. (He's a rabbi, remember. "Why does a rabbi always answer a question with another question?") He says, in effect, "My answer to your question is this: I tell the one among you who is without sin to cast the first stone." And suddenly they all realize, as Job did, that they had all along only *seemed* to be the questioners, the teachers, the judges, the testers, the controllers, the active ones, the knowing ones, like scientists examining some new species of animal. In reality they were and had always been the questioned ones, the students, the judged, the tested, the controlled, the ones who were acted upon, the known ones, not the knowing ones. They had always been this *because they are creatures*. God had always been testing them, not vice versa, every moment of their lives. What Christ did here was simply to snatch back the curtain of human ignorance for a moment so that all could see clearly for the first time what had always been happening throughout all of time.

No technique can accomplish this most radical epistemological breakthrough. Only His real presence can. That is why His methods can never be successfully imitated by any man. That is why no one can ever successfully imagine Him as a fictional character. No convincing fiction has ever been written about the most famous man in history. But much convincing fiction has been written about most of the other famous men in history, and much more will. Here is a strong argument for the truth of the Gospels, for Christianity: Christ could not possibly be fictional, for if no one in the world even now, after 2000 years of knowing Him, can write convincing fiction about Him, if no one can imagine "what would Jesus do" in a convincing way, as they can imagine what Alexander or Buddha or Augustine or Lincoln or Churchill would do, then how could a few Jewish fishermen

2000 years ago write such incredibly original, unprecedented creative fiction based on nothing? This character could not possibly have been invented because He still cannot be invented. He can only be real.

The way Jesus effects the role reversal between the questioner and the answerer cannot be put into a formula, because all formulae are universal and therefore repeatable, but Christ is the unique Son of God. It also cannot be put into a formula because all formulae are objective and impersonal, but Christ is the personal Subject, the divine I AM. He pulls off His "trick" repeatedly simply by being Himself, simply because it is His nature, as the sun pulls off its "trick" of shining simply because it is its nature to shine. Sunlight naturally illumines all things, things of all sizes, shapes, and colors, without effort. That's what light does because that's what light is. And this role reversal is what Christ keeps doing because I AM is what He is.

We see this role reversal happening again and again in the Gospels. We learn by repetition. The wise need fewer examples because they are quick to see the universal truth in the particular example. The wiser we are, the fewer examples we need. If we were really wise, if we had spiritual x-ray vision, we would discover that Jesus is divine from this one passage in John's Gospel alone. (In fact, this is exactly what happened to Arthur Katz, according to his autobiography, *Ben Israel*.)

After Jesus frees Himself from the condemnations of the scribes and Pharisees, He then frees the accused woman: "I do not condemn you." He does not send along the condemnation of the scribes and Pharisees to her but blocks it, and sends to her instead His liberation. They wanted to imprison Him as well as her in their logical trap. Instead, He frees her as well as Himself. Their work is to imprison, His is to free. For He is the Truth, and "the Truth shall make you free." (John 8:32)

Since God exists, nothing happens by chance. And since nothing happens by chance, God did not let this passage be put into John's Gospel by chance. It is not just about this woman but about all of us. We have all committed adultery against God. And as we read this passage, it is we who are being tested—not just by God's law against adultery, both physical and spiritual, but also by the story itself. The story tests us by asking us whose work we are doing, Christ's or the Pharisees? We may hope to remain spectators judging the spectacle from outside as we read this passage, but we cannot. We are drawn into the situation; we are not judging it but *we are being judged.* In fact we are always being judged, not just by the Law but by Christ. He is always the judging, knowing Subject, and we are always the judged, known objects. Our truth is our conformity to His knowledge.

For God does not discover truth, as we do. He decrees it, He creates it. We do this too, partially, in the creative arts. There, we make truth; elsewhere, we discover it. It is true that elves are small and impish in the world of *A Midsummer Night's Dream* because Shakespeare made them that way, and it is true that elves are tall and awesome in *The Lord of the Rings* because Tolkien made them that way. The creation (the universe) is God's art and man's science. What is objective to us (e.g. tigers) is subjective to God. First He invents tigers, then we discover them, as first Tolkien invents hobbits, then we discover them. When we discover truth about the creation, we are reading the thoughts of the Creator.

What does this theological truth have to do with John 8? It is the basis for Christ's liberation of the woman caught in adultery. For Christ is not a creature but the Creator. In the words of the Nicene Creed, He is "begotten, not made, consubstantial with the Father." The woman received the practical payoff of this theological mystery. And so do we. Christ is not passively imprisoned by truth, as we are; Christ actively liberates by truth, as God does. Christ is not a scientist but an artist.

Just connect these three verses and you will see: (1) "I am the Truth." (John 14:6) (2) "The truth shall make you free." (John 8:32) (3) "So if the Son makes you free, you are free indeed." (John 8:36)

But the story is only half over, and we like to forget the second half. Christ says not only "I forgive you" but also "Sin no more." Both are equally necessary parts of His work of liberation, like faith and works (the works of love) in salvation. Remember, the prophecy did not say that "His name shall be called 'Jesus' ['Savior,' or 'God saves'] because he will save his people from the *punishment* due to their sins," but "His name shall be called 'Jesus' because he shall save his people from their *sins*." Saying "I forgive you" but not "Sin no more" would have been just as much a work of imprisonment rather than liberation as the opposite, saying "Sin no more" but not "I forgive you," as the scribes and Pharisees did. For sin imprisons us just as certainly as unforgivingness does. "Whoever commits sin is the slave of sin." (John 8:34) "For the wages of sin is death, but the free gift of God is eternal life in Christ Jesus our Lord." (Romans 6: 23)

Sin is like a drug. To be freed from addiction to any drug, two things are necessary: someone has to love you tenderly enough to free you, and someone has to love you toughly enough to demand that you stay free. This is the Savior's double work. Sometimes theologians call it "justification" and "sanctification." The two cannot be separated. To separate the tender warp and the tough woof of this seamless garment is to unravel and destroy the whole of it. To oppose a "liberal" tenderness to a "conservative" toughness, or vice versa, is nothing but a new imprisonment, a new dilemma like the one the Pharisees posed to Jesus.

But Jesus escapes our dilemma too, as He escapes the Pharisees' dilemma. He escapes all our nets, for He is not a fish but the Fisherman, the "fisher of men," and we are His fish. To be caught in His net is to be freed, because His net is truth.

Thus, in the same chapter, after He frees the woman, He interprets what He has just done in telling us that "the truth will make you free" (vs.

32). But did the truth free her? Wasn't the truth that she had committed adultery? How could that truth free her?

We have difficulty seeing how that truth can free her because we think of "truth" as abstract and impersonal, as either a general principle (like "adultery is sin") or a particular fact (like "she has committed adultery"). Both general principles and particular facts are expressed in propositions, sentences, statements. This is "propositional truth."

I will not here play the popular card of trashing propositional truth. For propositional truth is precious, and is the servant, not the enemy, of Christ. That is why even propositional truth, even abstract truth, even philosophical truth, can be freeing.

For instance, the philosophy of Socrates frees us from much ignorance, especially from our ignorance about our own ignorance. But it does not free us from all ignorance. It tells us much about ourselves, but very little about God.

And the propositions of good psychology can free us from much self-deception. But not all. In fact, to think that it does is the greatest of self-deceptions.

And the propositions of science, philosophy's

child, and of technology, its grandchild, can free us from much ignorance about nature and much pain and suffering by "the conquest of nature." But we can only postpone, not conquer, nature's trump card, death.

The truths of science do increase our freedom. For instance, we are free to escape earth's gravity and travel through air or space only because of the propositional truths of physics and mathematics. But we cannot be free of gravity altogether, for it is in our very essence as material creatures. What goes up must come down eventually. No knowledge of abstract propositional truth can free us from that.

But Jesus can. He makes it possible to escape earth's gravity forever, to go up to Heaven and not down to Hell. He lifts our bodies from our graves and our souls from our sins.

How can He do that? Because He is the truth, and "the truth shall make you free," and "if the Son makes you free, you are free indeed." (John 8:36)

This is epistemology incarnated, and therefore empowered. He is "the word of power" because He is "the Word of God." He has the power to liberate the woman because He has the power to create the universe. He *is* the Word the Father spoke to create the universe. (Genesis 1:2) He is not just "the word *about* power" but "the word *of* power." (Luke 4:32; Hebrews 1:3) He does not merely copy what-is when He speaks; He creates what-is. When He says, "let there be life" at Lazarus's tomb, even death obeys Him.

He is "*the* Word of God" in the singular because He is absolutely singular. He is not "the word *about* God," not even the last word about God, but "the Word *of* God." He is not *about* anything else; everything else is about Him. Everything in the universe and everything in the Bible is a finger pointing to Him. He is the end of epistemology.

* * * * *

How do we know God? One indispensable way is to pray. And all prayer, if it is to reach the Father, must go through the Son, consciously or unconsciously, known or unknown. So Jesus is the way to know God here too.

Knowing persons requires words. How could Juliet ever know Romeo if no words ever passed between them? And how could you know God if He never spoke to you, through His inspired written Word and above all through the Word

Incarnate, and if you never spoke to Him, by prayer? Love needs words as well as music because love sings.

So prayer is necessary to know God (as distinct from knowing *about* God). But this is not the "necessity" of an obligation, one among many, like fitting a square into a quilt. This is *God* we're dealing with: the burning, blazing, bursting fire at the heart of all goodness and beauty and life. To pray is more like plunging yourself into a volcano than like fitting the missing piece into a jigsaw puzzle. Prayer is a matter of justice, but much more than that, it is a matter of love. To pray is not merely to give God His due, to perform your moral obligation, to fit something in; it is to touch the body of the God whose love spills out of five wounds as human blood.

III. Jesus' Anthropology

THE THIRD GREAT QUESTION of philosophy is the question of the questioner, the question of man. It is naturally third because after thinking about reality (metaphysics), we naturally think about our thinking (epistemology), and then about the thinkers, ourselves (anthropology).

But there is a "but." This division of philosophy is much more interesting than either metaphysics or epistemology; yet despite the intense interest, time, energy, and books that have been devoted to this pursuit, despite the fact that more than half of all the books on all the sciences that are sold in bookstores today are written about some aspect of psychology, there is no science with less agreement, less certainty, and less confidence that we now *know* what we used to not-know. We seem to know ourselves *less* well as a result of all this modern self-scrutiny than we did before. The more we look, the less we see. It is just the opposite with the external world. We can now understand the mysteries of the origin of the universe, 15 billion years ago, or the forces that keep the galaxies spinning trillions of light-years away, better than we can understand ourselves. "Know thyself," said Socrates, at the dawn of philosophy. But "know thyself" seems to be an unsolvable puzzle, a *koan*. We *cannot* know ourselves, yet we *must* know ourselves.

What does this have to do with Jesus, or Jesus with this? In the oft-repeated words of John Paul II, "Jesus alone shows man to himself." Since He is both perfect God and perfect Man, He perfectly reveals both God and man. Jesus is the solution to the *koan*.

But an answer is only as meaningful as the question. We need to understand why this question is a *koan* before we can appreciate the uniqueness of Jesus' solution to it.

"Know thyself" seems to be an unsolvable *koan*. It is. We cannot solve this problem because it is not a problem at all, it is a mystery (to use Gabriel Marcel's useful distinction): we are involved in it, not detached from it. This problem "encroaches upon its own data." We cannot solve this problem because we *are* this problem. As the eye can see any object, but not itself, so the mind can know any object, but not itself, because it is not an object.

When we look at ourselves, we get in our own way. We stand in our own light and make our own shadow. Then we identify ourselves with our shadow, the shadow we have cast, or the image of ourselves that we have cast in the mirror. But that is not the self; that is an image or a shadow *of* the self.

We are like spectators at a play whose very presence and gaze affects and alters the players and the play. For we are not only the spectators; we are also the players. In science, this is called the "observer effect": we alter the thing observed by the very act of observing it. Whether or not that principle applies to subatomic particles, it certainly applies to us. For we alone in the universe are subjects, not objects. In man for the first time the universe achieves self-consciousness. We are selves, subjects, *who*s, not things, objects, *what*s. How can we make a subject of knowledge into an object of knowledge? How can the archer become his own target? How can the *I* become an *it* without ceasing to be an *I*?

Clearly, it cannot. And clearly, it must. We cannot know ourselves, yet we must know ourselves.

That is our *koan*. We must know ourselves because if we do not, then we do not know who it is that is knowing anything else at all. If we do not sign the impressively large bank account of our knowledge, *we* do not possess a penny of it.

In Zen Buddhism, a *koan* is a puzzle that is in principle not solvable by ordinary, rational thought. Its purpose is to put to death, or put to sleep, ordinary thought so as to release "Buddha-mind," which is thought without a subject-object dualism. The sudden emergence of this radically new kind of thought is "Enlightenment," or *satori,* the Zen version of *Nirvana* ("blowing-out" the candle fire of ordinary thought).

I do not believe in this Buddhist goal, for as a Christian I believe in God and in Creation, and therefore in the reality of the subject-object dualism that Buddhism seeks to overcome. The whole universe is objective to God. The subject-object dualism, or the I-it dualism, that Buddhism seeks to overcome is really the Creator-creature dualism, since the Creator's name is "I AM" and His creatures are His objects. There is another subject-object dualism that Buddhism denies: the one between the objects in the universe and us human subjects, who bear God's image and are therefore also I's, or subjects. The two things Christ reveals to man, God and man, the two subjects, are the two things Buddhism denies.

But even though I do not believe in the truth of the Buddhist answer, I do believe in the profundity of the Buddhist question, and in the power of a *koan* to transform consciousness. I also believe that God Himself set us a *koan* in making us insatiably curious about ourselves while at the same time making those selves inaccessible to ordinary curiosity.

He made us in His own image as *I*'s (subjects, persons)—and yet at the same time *it*'s (objects, creatures). We are metaphysically dual, double.

It seems that we cannot overcome this dualism except by denying the reality of either or both of its horns: the Western materialist reduces personality to a thing among other things in the world while the Eastern mystic reduces the objective reality of things, including our own finite thinghood, to consciousness, or spirit, or "the Buddha-mind," or Brahman ("thou art That").

Down through the ages, our most brilliant philosophers have been drawn to one or the other of those two classic errors in anthropology: either materialistic naturalism or spiritualist pantheism, either confusing Man with things or with God. Incredible!—our greatest philosophers, our greatest knowers, do not know themselves well enough to avoid confusing their very essence with what they are not!

And when our philosophers do avoid the two extreme errors of materialism and pantheism, they still fall into a modified form of one or the other: animalism or angelism. If they do not confuse us with matter or with God, they confuse us with animals or with angels. Empiricists, positivists, pragmatists, and secularists are scandalized by the soul, the supernatural, miracles, Heaven, and abstract universal truths. They are the animalists. Platonists, Gnostics, Cartesians, New Age flakes, and those who seek "spirituality" instead of sanctity in their religion are the angelists. They are scandalized by the body, the natural, the Incarnation, the sacraments, the visible Church, and the concrete.

Christ is the answer to this dilemma. He is the definitive refutation of both errors (for, remember, Christ reveals to us not only perfect God but also perfect Man). Christ is not just the perfect anthropologist; He is perfect *anthropos*. He is what anthropology is all about. He is man as man is designed to be. He is not the freak; we are the freaks.

The greatest modern Christian anthropologist philosopher was Pope John Paul II. At the center of his philosophy was anthropology, and at the center of his anthropology was Christ. "Christ is the meaning of man," he kept repeating. And therefore "in reality, it is only in the mystery of the Word made flesh that the mystery of man truly becomes clear." John Paul loved to quote that sentence, from the documents of Vatican II (see *Catechism of the Catholic Church* [hereafter CCC] 359). What we fail to see in our own philosophies and psychologies and anthropologies about ourselves, we see in Christ: our own meaning and destiny. He is an x-ray mirror: when we look at Him, we see our own depth.

Christ is the answer to the question: What is the meaning of human life? Who are we meant to be? The answer is that we are destined to be little Christs. The meaning of life is to be Christ. The answer to the primary question of anthropology is not any abstract ideal but a concrete, realized fact. The meaning of Man is *a* man, *this* man.

The Old Testament told us that we are created by God in His own image (Genesis 1:26–27), but only the New Testament fully shows us what that image is: it is Christ. It is this, rather than some vague humanism, that St. Ignatius Loyola meant by saying that "the glory of God is a man fully alive." (All Jesuits, please *nota bene*!) "A man fully alive" means "a little Christ."

How could we miss it? Only because we are more than half asleep more than half the time. The New Testament says it strongly and clearly in many places. For instance, Romans 8:29: "Those whom he foreknew, he also predestined to be conformed to the image of his Son, in order that he might be the first-born among many brethren." Or I Corinthians 15:49: "Just as we have borne the image of the man of dust, we shall also bear the image of the man of heaven." Or II Peter 1:4: "He has granted to us his precious and very great promises, that through these you may . . . become partakers of the divine nature."

There is also a second reason why we need the divine revelation of Christ to know ourselves: because "without the knowledge revelation gives of God, we cannot recognize sin clearly, and are tempted to explain it as merely a developmental flaw, a psychological weakness, a mistake, or the necessary consequence of an inadequate social structure." (CCC 389). Christ shows us how *abnormal* we are by being the norm. If we let Him judge us rather than us judging Him, we see that our "normal" is really abnormal. That is the crucial epistemological question in anthropology: do we judge Christ or does Christ judge us?

Without knowing Christ, and thus knowing our "abnormalism," we must fall into the fundamental error of "normalism." All secular psychology, sociology, and anthropology is fundamentally askew at its very foundation because it assumes, wrongly, that its object, man, is in his natural state. All its data are its observations of "normal" human behavior, just as in physics or astronomy all the data come from observations of how matter naturally behaves. Just imagine how radically physics would change if physicists came to believe that gravity was not inherent to matter at all but that matter had "fallen" into this abnormal state at some time in the past. Imagine the radical shock astronomy would experience if astronomers came to believe that stars only started to shine at some point in past time called the "fall." Christianity reveals a shock as great as that in anthropology in its doctrine of the Fall, in its most basic interpretation of human history, in which the three great defining events are Creation, Fall, and Redemption.

Christianity adds two men to its database that secular anthropology does not know: Adam and Christ, the only two innocent men who have ever lived, and Christianity judges fallen men by that norm. Without that corrective, we inevitably think backwards and misunderstand our present sinfulness as natural and normal, and thus see innocence, and even sainthood, as abnormal and unnatural, superhuman rather than human. In the same way, drunks and drug addicts see sober people as abnormal. We are all morally drunk and sin addicts. So it was quite natural for Bill Clinton's supporters to claim that it was wrong and even immoral for his critics to expect of presidents "unrealistic, unattainable" moral virtues like fidelity and honesty.

This is the most fundamental error of our secular society's view of man, and the root of all its other errors. "Ignorance of the fact that man has a wounded nature inclined to evil gives rise to serious errors in the areas of education, politics, social action, and morals." (CCC 401) In all four fields, secular "liberalism" (a misleading term because it is not really liberating) denies the reality of personal sin and sees man as a lettuce rather than a potato. (Lettuce rots from the outside in; potatoes rot from the inside out.) So their solution is always a "lettuce solution": let us do this or that, let us improve the social environment, let us throw some money at the social structures, or let us condition people by better education. They are like the Pharisees, who clean the outside but ignore the rot within. (Matthew 23:25–26) Someone defined a liberal as one who demands the right to breathe clean air so he can speak dirty words.

The only way to correct this skewered perspective is to find the true reference point. But we can't! "Physician, heal thyself." We are the cripple in the commercial: "I've fallen and I can't get up." We can't go back to paradise. The words of the song are exactly wrong: "And the riders will not stop us 'cause the only drug they'll find is Paradise" No, the riders (the cops) *will* stop us because they will find every other drug *but* that one.

We cannot go back to Paradise to see unfallen Adam. "But we see Jesus." (Hebrews 2:9) Christ is our new data for anthropology. Christ is our standard, or norm.

Without this data we are like a dog in a cage at the airport who has chewed off his dog tag so that he does not know his true name, or the name of his master, or his home. He does not know where he has come from, who he is, or where he is destined to go.

"Without Jesus Christ we do not know the meaning of our life, or our death, of our God or of our selves." (Pascal) We get this crucial fourfold information only from Christ. Our true name is "Christ's brother, God's adopted child." We must keep this dog tag, cherish it, live by it, remember it, read it often. The tag is Christ. Christ is the key to anthropology.

But how can we become Christs? Is this not another impossible *koan?* We must become Christs, but we cannot. Not all our prayers and sighs and tears, not all our loves and thoughts and deeds and mystical experiences, can do that. We simply can't do it. To do it, we have to become someone else. We have to be "born again." Of all the images for change among all the world's teachers, Jesus' image here (in John 3) stands out as the most radical one of all. So much so that Nicodemus argued that it was simply impossible: "How can such things be?"

> Now there was a man of the Pharisees named Nicodemus, a ruler of the Jews.
> This man came to Jesus by night and said to him, "Rabbi, we know that you are a teacher come from God, for no one can do these signs that you do unless God is with him." Jesus answered him, "Truly, truly I say

to you, unless one is born anew, he cannot see the kingdom of God." Nicodemus said to him, "How can a man be born when he is old? Can he enter a second time into his mother's womb and be born?" Jesus answered,

"Truly, truly I say to you, unless one is born of water and the Spirit, he cannot enter the kingdom of God. That which is born of the flesh is flesh, and that which is born of the Spirit is spirit. Do not marvel that I said to you, 'You must be born anew.' The wind blows where it wills, and you hear the sound of it, but you do not know whence it comes or whither it does. So it is with everyone who is born of the Spirit." Nicodemus said to him, "How can this be?" Jesus answered him, "Are you a teacher of Israel, and yet you do not understand this?" (John 3:1–10)

Nicodemus came to Jesus with two questions in his mind: about the Messiah and about the "kingdom of God." According to the prophets, the Messiah would bring about this kingdom on earth, and Jesus had been preaching about the kingdom, so was he the Messiah or not? And if so, how could we enter this "kingdom of God"?

Nicodemus seems to have prepared a little flattering speech. He began politely and indirectly, with a word of praise for Jesus' miracles ("signs"): "Rabbi, we know that you are a teacher from God, for no one can do the miracles you do unless God is with him." This was a polite, roundabout way of asking: Are you the Messiah? It probably would have taken Nicodemus five more minutes of flattery to get to the second question, the practical question, the "bottom line" question about how to enter this kingdom of God. But Jesus cut through all the flattery and immediately answered the question that lay on Nicodemus' heart, without waiting for the question to rise to Nicodemus' lips: "Truly, truly I say to you, unless a man is born anew, he cannot see the kingdom of God."

Nicodemus is startled. Jesus startles three different kinds of people, and thus reveals three different kinds of startles relative to Jesus. Everything is relative to Jesus. He is the best standard for judging anything, including people and their startles. In fact, these three startles are a clue to a basic anthropology, a basic classification of people into three classes. Pascal defines these three classes as follows: "There are only three kinds of people: those who seek God and have found him—and these are both reasonable and happy—those who are seeking God and have not yet found Him—and these are reasonable and unhappy—and those who neither seek God nor find Him—and these are both unreasonable and unhappy." (*Pensées* 160) Jesus startles His disciples, who have found Him, in one way. He startles Nicodemus, who is seeking Him but has not yet found Him, in another way. And He startles His enemies, who neither seek Him nor find Him, in a third way.

Those who become His disciples and are "born again" of the Spirit have the same ability to startle the world that Jesus had. It is an invisible power like the wind, a power that can overturn a whole pagan Empire, the greatest in world history, as a hurricane can overturn a forest. That's why the world called His disciples "those men who have turned the world upside down." (Acts 17:6)

Nicodemus asks Jesus to explain His startling image. Surely He does not mean it literally, for that is a physical impossibility. Nor could He be referring to reincarnation, which no Jew believed, for it would imply that the individual is not God's unique created image, a finite "I" that is as uniquely individual, in its finite way, as God, the infinite "I AM." So Nicodemus believes that Jesus' image must be a mere figure of speech, a rhetorical exaggeration. But he wonders: what does it mean, literally?

Jesus' interpretation of his image is even more startling than the initial image. It is not to water it down ("it's only an image") but to repeat it with the Rabbinical formula "Truly, truly I say to you", which means "You must interpret these words in the strongest possible sense, not the weakest. It is more than literally true, not less."

Then He adds an explanation: the identity of the parent: it is not Mother Earth and matter, but it is the Spirit of Father God and the water of baptism: "unless one is born of water and the Spirit he cannot enter the kingdom."

So this rebirth is spiritual, not fleshly. But that does not make it merely symbolic, less real, a mere image. Just the opposite: the Spirit is *more* real, more solid and substantial, than the perishable flesh. So spiritual birth is more solid and substantially real than physical birth.

Jesus then compares fleshly and spiritual birth by explaining that the child resembles the parent in both cases: "flesh begets flesh, Spirit begets spirit." It is startling yet utterly reasonable. But seeing the uncomprehending look on Nicodemus' face, Jesus says, ironically, "You are supposed to be a teacher in Israel, a teacher of God's revealed mysteries, and yet you yourself do not understand this? That is the whole point and purpose of Israel."

He then compares this unfamiliar thing with a familiar thing, the wind. The wind is a natural symbol for the Spirit. The same word, in both Hebrew (*ruah'*) and Greek (*pneuma*) means "spirit," "wind," and "breath of life." The wind is quite invisible, yet quite real. And though the *origin* of the wind is as invisible as the wind itself, its *effects* are not. And these can be radical. A great wind can blow down houses and trees. The same is true of the wind of the Spirit: it can blow down the greatest kingdom of this world, the universal ("catholic") Roman Empire, and it can erect another kingdom, which is "not of this world": the universal ("Catholic") Roman Church.

You cannot see the wind, but you can see *that there is a wind* by seeing its effects, by reading the wind's fingerprints, so to speak. Unless, of course, you are hypnotized by the modern idiocy of materialism, the fallacy that the trees make the wind, that visible things cause invisible things and not vice versa.

We habitually think of the invisible as abstract and impersonal, as a set of ideas or ideals, words or principles. And we think of only the visible as concretely alive and life-changing and dangerous, like tigers or cancers or surgeons. But God's Spirit is much *more* alive and fiery, and He is the ultimate agent in every baby's conception as well as in every believer's conversion. The Holy Spirit is not an "it" but a "He": a Person, not a Force. He is as shatteringly real and as revolutionary as a hurricane.

And Jesus will send Him to all who will open the door of their heart to Him. And if you open your door to that wind, He will radically rearrange the furniture of your house.

So the image of being "born again" is not too strong but too weak. The difference between being born again and not being born again is even more radical than the difference between being born and not being born. For the difference between being born and not being born is a difference between temporal being and temporal nonbeing in this world, but the difference between being born again and not being born again is a difference between eternal being and eternal nonbeing, Heaven and Hell. It is an absolute difference, like the difference between being pregnant and not being pregnant. It is not a relative difference, like the difference between being very good and being very bad. It is not simply an addition or an improvement to your life: it is life itself. It is not the difference between more life and less life, or good life and bad life, but between life and death. Therefore it cannot be brought about by trying a little harder, or a lot harder, or by being very good, or sincere, or nice. It is a gift, just as new physical life is a gift. It is the gift of a new *being*. It is the transition from non-being to being. It is an act of creation. Only God can create (*bara'*).

But to do this, to make us pregnant with His new life, God must be as really present to us as a man is to a woman to make her pregnant. There are no pregnancies by email. You can't get pregnant simply by thinking about it, or by a "transformation of consciousness," however profound it may be. Your body can get pregnant with human life only by the real presence of a man inside your body, and your soul can get pregnant with divine life only by the real presence of God inside your soul.

And Jesus is that real presence of God to man. He was visibly present in His individual human body for thirty-three years in first-century Israel, but He is just as really present, though invisibly, in His universal Body of the Church, the "mystical Body of Christ," for the rest of history throughout the world. The Church is "the extension of the

Incarnation." That is why She not only teaches in His name and with His authority but also baptizes in His name, forgives sins in His name, offers the Eucharist in His name and real presence.

This is not optional. This is the way. Unless you are born again, you cannot enter God's kingdom. Unless you get pregnant with God, you cannot go to Heaven. This is not Southern Baptist Fundamentalism; it is Jesus of Nazareth Christianity.

But like Nicodemus, many of us still just don't get it. We miss the very center and essence of this whole religion business. We think it's about thinking differently, believing differently, evaluating differently, acting differently, and forget that the root of all of these things is *being* differently. Christ came to give us not just new thoughts and values but new being.

Just as many of us, like Nicodemus, just don't get the heart of the religion business, many of us don't get the heart of the sex business. Just as the main point and purpose of religion is creation (the creation of new, divine being), the main point and purpose of sex is procreation. But we've turned pregnancy into an "accident"! That's like accepting religion, faith, creed, church, sacraments, the whole package, and then calling your entrance into Heaven an accident! Or like eating healthy food and calling your body's health an accident. We're not just stupid; we're twisted!

When Jesus told Nicodemus that "unless you are born again, you cannot see the Kingdom of God," Nicodemus was amazed, and voiced his amazement: "Can such things be?" This is a candid, honest, humble reaction. Nicodemus was a Pharisee, and they weren't all bad. His voice is very different from the voice we hear from most of the other Pharisees in the New Testament. But not all; not Gamaliel (see Acts 5:34–39) or Paul (see Philippians 3:5). Nicodemus' amazement is the amazement of an honest child not hiding behind a mask of high office, reputation, and supposed expertise. The mask is off. Nicodemus is now like Socrates, not worried about appearances but only about reality and truth.

Jesus' answer to Nicodemus' amazement is another kind of amazement. Jesus is amazed that Nicodemus is amazed. Jesus' reaction to Nicodemus' utterly non-ironic surprise is ironic surprise: "What's this? You are a rabbi, a teacher of Israel, and you don't know *this*? This is what all of Israel and all of Judaism is *for*.

"All the laws and the prophets, all your scriptures, all your history, so full of prophets, providence, and miracles, all this 2000 year long divine teaching program, starting with Abraham, in fact all the covenants, starting with Adam and Noah, was for *this*. This is the end My Father had in mind when He chose Israel. He chose her to be a womb within humanity for a second birth of humanity. This was His intention from the beginning, from the Creation of the universe. This is the point of everything, of stars and galaxies, of geological and biological evolution. The highest purpose of the material universe He created is to supply the dust He used to form mankind from (Genesis 2:7), to be the womb for mankind's first, physical birth. This was the womb that He designed to give birth to women's wombs, which in turn give birth to new men and women, new persons with immortal souls, made in His image. That was the first point of the universe: people. Did you think God cared about gases and galaxies? They were just the preparation, the preliminary, the placenta for people. People are the point of the universe. The universe 'peoples' as a flower bush flowers.

"And within this humanity, the point of Israel was to be a second womb, a womb within the womb of the world. And the ultimate point and product of this chosen womb is the Messiah, and he is speaking to you at this moment face to face. The whole meaning of Israel is me, and you, the teacher of Israel, do not know me. How ironic!

"And within Israel there is a third womb, my mother. She is all Israel come to one single, sharp point, like a pen: a young virgin kneeling at her prayers, addressed by my angel, who breathlessly waited to see whether my chosen door into humanity and its salvation would freely open or not. And it did. She said yes. I knew she would. I am the only man in history who chose his own mother.

"So the universe was a womb for humanity, and humanity was a womb for Israel, and Israel was a womb for Mary, and Mary was a womb for me. Thus, Mary is the point of the universe, and I am the point of that point."

All of this, not one bit less, is implied in Jesus' claim. To unpack that much took 2000 years, and to unpack it *all* will take thousands more—no, it will take eternity. The Church has only begun to unpack her holy luggage, her "deposit of faith." From the perspective of the year A.D. 5000, we will be "the primitive Christians."

At each step in this design of God, the role of

the Spirit is essential. The Spirit breathed order into chaos (Genesis 1:2) and life into man (Genesis 2:7). We are made in God's image because we have God's breath (Spirit). And when we defaced the image of God in us by sin, God's response was to send the Spirit to call up the miracle of Israel and finally to conceive Mary in her mother Anna's womb without Original Sin, and then to conceive Christ in Mary's womb without a human father. The Spirit was Christ's food and strength and wisdom throughout His earthly life. And His gift of His and His Father's Spirit to us is the culminating point of His ministry (see John 16:7). The Spirit's work is this "new birth" that Jesus speaks of to Nicodemus. The Spirit fulfills David's prophetic prayer in Psalm 51: "Create in me a clean heart, O God, and put a new and right spirit within me." Only God can create (*bara'*), can make something out of nothing, can bridge the infinite gap between nonbeing and being. God creates a new human spirit (a soul) at conception every time physical love provides an open body, and He creates a new spirit, a real human participation in His own divine life, every time spiritual love and faith provide an open soul. The door for new natural human life (*bios*) to enter the world is a woman saying Yes to a man by sexual intercourse; the door for new supernatural, eternal life (*zoe*) to enter the world is a soul saying Yes to God by faith, as Mary did. The promise to her is also to us: "The Holy Spirit shall come upon you, and the power of the Most High shall overshadow you; therefore the holy thing that will be born of you will be called the Son of God." (Luke 1:35)

This is the real meaning and purpose of history; this is the true "short history of time": our "new birth" into eternal life, our becoming little Christs, children of God, with our divine Father's divine nature as well as our human parents' human nature—in a word, having two natures, human and divine, like Christ (though our divine nature is only by grace, by adoption, and by participation). For this is any parent's first and primary gift to the child: the very nature of the parent. This gift is the foundation of all others: love, time, education.

And that is the point of religion that Nicodemus did not know. He knew everything except the one thing most worth knowing, the reason for everything else that has ever happened. And that reason is sitting right in front of him.

And of us.

IV. Jesus' Ethics

OF ALL THE GREAT questions of philosophy that all men by nature ask in all times, places, and cultures, the ethical, or moral, question is the most necessary one, the most practical one, the most interesting one, the most personal one, the one that holds us eye to eye and demands an answer. How should we then live? What is the greatest good, the highest value, the meaning of life? How can I avoid the tragedy of getting A's in all my subjects but flunking life?

Of the four great philosophical questions, this is the one that everyone knows has something to do with Christ. Even those who do not believe His claim to be the Lord usually praise His morality, both His preaching and His practice. He is by a wide margin the most admired and influential moral teacher of all time. But what is distinctive, what is different, what is new about His answer to the moral question?

His morality was *not* new. There is no such thing as a new morality, only new immoralities. Everyone always knew what was good and what was evil. No sane individual and no sane society ever believed that justice, charity, honesty, self-control, mercy, loyalty, and wisdom were wicked or immoral, or that injustice, hatred, lying, addiction, cruelty, betrayal, and folly were moral goods or obligations. Jesus' morality was only the fullest flower of the plant that God had already planted in the nature of man, in all human hearts and consciences by creating us in His image.

Conscience is universal. It exists in all men. In some it is horribly weak, and in some it seems almost dead, but it never is. A man totally without a conscience is not a man, just as a man without a mind at all is not a man. (A man with an I.Q. of 45 is a man; a man with an I.Q. of 0 is not.)

Jesus' moral appeals, therefore, were appeals to a moral conscience that was already there. The ground had already been fertilized. And other sowers had sown moral seeds in that field, and many of them had sown very deep and lively seeds, though no one had ever sowed so many deep seeds in so few words as Jesus. If you look at Jesus' Jewish tradition you will find that there is hardly any moral saying of Jesus in the Gospels whose equivalent cannot be found somewhere in the scriptures or in the sayings of the rabbis. Much of it, even some of the most startling points about humility and self-sacrifice and the power of weakness, can also be found outside Judaism: in Lao Tzu, in Buddha, in Confucius, or in Socrates. So what's new? What new moral doors does the Golden Key open?

There are really *three* moral questions, three basic parts to morality: how should we relate to each other, to ourselves, and to God? How should my ship cooperate with the other ships in the fleet, how should it stay shipshape itself, and what is the fleet's mission? These three questions are the question of social morality, the question of individual morality, and the question of the meaning of life. The last one is the most important because the answer to it makes a difference to the answer to all the others. It is the question of the ultimate end of everything else. Everything else is ultimately a means to this final end. And though "the end does not justify the means"—that is, a good end does not justify an evil means—yet a good end does justify a good means, for the means are relative to the end. That's what a means *means:* a "means" *to an end.*

So what is Jesus' answer to the question of the meaning of life, the ultimate end, the greatest good?

The answer is Christ Himself. Christ is the greatest good.

How then should we live? What sort of people should we be? Christs. We should be little Christs. We must "grow into the full measure of the stature of Christ." (Ephesians 3:14)

And how should we treat each other? As Christs. "Truly, truly I say to you, whatever you do to one of these least of my brethren, you do to me." (Matthew 25:40)

You see, instead of *telling* us the answer, Christ *shows* us the answer, for He *is* the answer. He shows us Himself.

That's what's new, this New Man. We all knew the other answers. We have never lived morality very well, but we have always known it quite well, quite adequately. Contrast how well we know morality with how well we know metaphysics, or epistemology, or anthropology—or, certainly, theology. God has left us to make many mistakes in those other areas, but God has not left Himself without clear witness in the area of morality. He has given every one of us two heavenly prophets of morality who speak powerfully to each of us if only we listen. Each of us has a conscience, and each of us has an angel. Each of us has two prophets from God, an inner prophet and an outer prophet.

With all this help, the map of moral principles is so clear that even an idiot can read it. (Applying those principles to complex and changing situations, of course, is a complex, changing, and not-so-simple task.) We do not have too few principles in our many moral philosophies; we have too many. We need to see the oneness of all of them. And we see that when we see Jesus. We see that there is "only one thing needful" (Luke 10:42), and that is Him. We do not need "Jesus and" but "Jesus only" (Matthew 17:8). In Him are all goods, all gifts, absolutely everything we need. (Philippians 4:19). For when we know Him, we learn that we do not really need many of the little good things we think we need, the many Martha-things, like making sure the supper is always on the table on time. And when we know Him, we learn that we do need one thing that we thought we did not need: the Mary-thing, simply sitting at His feet and listening and loving. He is really all we need. Literally. Besides Him, the only other thing we need to know is that besides Him there is no other thing we need to know.

St. Paul teaches this scandalously simple idea of the good life as simply Christ. His formula for the good life could not possibly be simpler: "For me to live is Christ." (Philippians 1:21). And therefore he goes on to say next that "to die is gain," for if life is Christ, then death is only more Christ.

About half of the words Jesus spoke in the Gospels are about ethics. Yet Jesus' most world-changing work in ethics is not his words, which are many, but Himself, which is one. He is not called "the words of God" but "the Word of God."

He is the world's greatest moral teacher, but He is more than that. He is the world's most perfect moral example, but He is more than that. He is the world's greatest prophet, but He is more than that. He is more than one who taught goodness and lived goodness and demanded goodness. He *is* goodness.

On one occasion someone addressed Him as "good master," and He asked him, "Why do you call me good? No one is truly good except God." (Matthew 19:17) He was not denying that He was God but affirming it, and thus affirming that He was more than a good man, even more than a "good master." He is not just *a* good man, He is the whole of goodness, goodness incarnate, the universal good, not just a partial or particular good. He is not just the best teacher of the meaning of life; He *is* the meaning of life. Buddha says, "Look not to me, look to my teaching"; Jesus says, "Come unto Me." (Matthew 11:28) He is not just one who perfectly exemplifies the meaning of life, He *is* the meaning of life. He is not an example of anything. Examples point beyond themselves, but He does not just *point out* the good way, He *is* the good way. He does not just speak the truth about goodness, He *is* the truth about goodness. He does not just live the good life, He *is* the good life. "I AM the way, and the truth, and the life." (John 14:6)

This is so shocking that it looks like what analytic philosophers of language would call "a category confusion," as if Plato had said that the eternal Essence of Beauty Itself was in his kitchen preparing dinner, or that Justice was six feet tall.

The point is hard to see because it is so simple, so single. Since our minds and hearts are *not* simple, it will be easier for us to see the point if we make it more complex. So let's split it into four parts, or four points, or four dimensions: first, the "personalism" of following Him instead of a set of impersonal principles; second, the overcoming of legalism by this simplicity; third, the refutation of moral relativism, which is the apparent opposite of legalism; and fourth, the secret of moral success.

1. Jesus' Personalism: Seeing "Jesus Only"

> And after six days Jesus took with him Peter and James and John his brother, and led them up a high mountain apart. And he was transfigured before them, and his face shone like the sun, and his garments became white as light. And behold, there appeared to them Moses and Elijah, talking with him. And Peter said to Jesus, "Lord, it is well that we are here; if you wish, I will make three booths here, one for you and one for Moses and one for Elijah." He was still speaking when lo, a bright cloud over-shadowed them, and a voice from the cloud said, "This is my beloved Son, with whom I am well pleased; listen to him." When the disciples heard this, they fell on their faces and were filled with awe. But Jesus came and touched them, saying, "Rise, and have no fear." And when they lifted up their eyes, they saw no one but Jesus only. (Matthew 17:8)

The first thing to get clear about this "transfiguration" is that it was not a transfiguration of Jesus' reality but of the disciples' vision. Jesus did not change and become brighter than light. He always was and is brighter than light. (He is not a little bit like light; light is a little bit like Him.) It was the disciples' eyes that were changed. God enabled them to see what is instead of just what appears. He lifted the curtain.

It is exactly like the scene in II Kings 6, when the wicked king of Syria finds out where the prophet Elisha is staying, and sends troops to kill him:

> It was told him, "Behold, he is in Dothan." So he sent there horses and chariots and a great army; and they came by night and surrounded the city. When the servant of the man of God [Elisha] rose early in the morning and went out, behold, an army with horses and chariots was round about the city. And the servant said, "Alas, my master! What shall we do?" He [Elisha] said, "Fear not, for those who are with us are more than those who are with them." Then Elisha prayed. "O Lord, I pray thee, open his eyes that he may see." So the Lord opened the eyes of the young man, and he saw, and behold, the mountain was full of horses and chariots of fire about Elisha.

God did not put this vision of the fiery army of angels into Elisha's servant's eyes. He simply removed the scales from his eyes. (Angels aren't there only when we see them!)

God did something similar to Peter, James, and John on the Mount of Transfiguration. Just before this, Peter had found it difficult to see "Jesus only" when He walked on the dark and fearful waters of the storm at sea (Matthew 14), and he began to sink when he took his eyes off Jesus. Now Peter also finds it difficult to see "Jesus only" atop the mountain in the bright heavenly glory. (Matthew 17) For he blurts out the ridiculous but reasonable-sounding proposal to build three shrines. If Jesus had allowed this, it would have become a tourist trap in a few centuries, and Peter would be famous as a developer instead of a disciple. What is ridiculous is not the idea of building shrines, but building three of them, putting Jesus in the same category as Moses and Elijah. And Peter probably thought this was flattery! God corrects Peter by a voice from Heaven that says, in effect, "Who do you think this is, anyway? I have many servants, but only one Son." (Matthew 17:5)

How did foolish Peter and the others manage to become so wise as to see "Jesus only"? Very simply: as soon as the voice of God commanded, "Listen to Him," they obeyed. "They fell on their faces and were filled with awe." (Matthew 17:6) (We live in a horribly impoverished age when this most basic religious emotion strikes our teachers as primitive and our students as incomprehensible.) Only because the disciples obeyed did they experience the holy fear, and only because they experienced the holy fear could Jesus come and touch them and say, "Fear not." Fear is the necessary precondition for "fear not." "The fear of the Lord is the beginning of wisdom." (Proverbs 9:10) And this is moral wisdom, the wisdom of holiness. (See Job 28:28)

We usually think wisdom comes first and leads to holiness, but it is the opposite. We think we must first see and then act, but it is the opposite. We think the will follows the mind, but it is the opposite. We are Greeks instead of Jews. The Jews knew that it was the other way round, that moral obedience comes first, and then, after we obey, our sight is clarified. Only wills open to obedience can give us eyes open to wisdom. Thus Jesus says, "If your will were to do the will of my Father, you would understand my teaching." (John 7:17)

And thus was the disciples' sight clarified by their obedience. What was the clarification? Simply that "when they lifted up their eyes they saw Jesus only." That is wisdom: to see "Jesus only." The only way to attain this advanced wisdom of seeing "Jesus only" is to begin with the primitive wisdom of the fear of the Lord and obedience to His voice.

What does it mean to see "Jesus only"? The "only" here is not the exclusive "only" but the inclusive "only." It is not Jesus outside of all things but Jesus inside all things; not Jesus excluding all things but Jesus including all things. For "grace perfects nature" rather than destroying it. God empowers His children, like a great father who is willing to appear small so that His children can appear great. He does not rival His children, like a small father who is worried about appearing great and therefore makes his children appear small. God does not belittle us, He "be-greats" us.

The ultimate reason why grace perfects nature is that God is love, and love does not harm or rival or destroy or displace anything at all. Jesus does not displace Moses or Elijah or Peter or Judaism ("I came not to destroy the Law and the Prophets but to fulfill them"—Matthew 5:17). The supremely concrete proof of this principle is Christ Himself, in Whom divinity (grace) perfectly perfects humanity (nature).

He does come to destroy something, though: sin. He is the Lord of life and therefore the enemy of the enemy of life, which is sin. He kills only that which kills and therefore needs to be killed. We all know that we harbor and cherish some enemy of life, of *our* life, some habitual sin, or even something innocent in itself that He sees leads to sin for us, or keeps us from fuller life: some creature comfort, some security blanket, some earthly happiness—perhaps biological life itself—that will build up a shell around us and make His entrance more difficult, make it harder for us to receive the fullness of life and joy in the end because of this lesser life now. So the divine gardener prunes us, killing the lesser life to grow the greater.

Since He kills the lesser life, which is part of nature, it looks as if His grace does not perfect nature but destroys it. But it does perfect nature, for the result of the death is a greater life. The pruned bush naturally doubts the good intentions of the gardener. But if it lets itself be pruned now, in faith, it will see next year why it was right to trust the gardener. It's not true that "seeing is believing" but it is true that "believing is seeing." As Jesus said at Lazarus' tomb, "See? Didn't I tell you that if you believed, you would see?" (John 11:40)

Of course we cannot see the end from the beginning, as He can. We do not see the perfect plant we will become by His pruning, nor do we see the Gardener: "No man has seen God at any time" (John 1:18). "But we see Jesus" (Hebrews 2:9). We see "Jesus only" (Matthew 17:8) And if we take our eyes off Him, we are like a little child who sees only the scoop of ice cream fall from the cone onto the ground, and who wails in agony as if this were an unredeemable tragedy. The child just has to take his eyes off the ice cream and look trustingly at Daddy, who gave it to him.

That's the best thing we can do: look at Jesus. That's what Mary did and Martha didn't. And when we look to Him for help because we have real or apparent needs, whether big or little, whether falling World Trade Centers or falling ice cream cones, the best thing He can tell us is what He told Job: "Just trust Me, child. Know yourself and know Me. I am the giver of 'every good and perfect gift' (James 1:17), and you are only a child who cannot understand My designs. Your wisdom is trust, my wisdom is providence. For you are only you, and I am I. I am not man and you are not God. Why is it so hard for you to remember that elementary fact? Let me help you remember: tell me, 'where were you when I designed your world?'" (Job 38:4)

This is Lesson One: that we do not know. If we do not know that, we do not know anything else. God taught Lesson One to Job, and also to Socrates.

And then Jesus taught us Lesson Two, which is the *answer* to Lesson One's question "Where were you when I designed your world?" He says, "I will tell you where you were: you were in the center of my vision and at the center of my heart. I designed the universe *for you,* for your highest good and greatest joy, which is also my greatest glory and my greatest joy. My greatest joy is you, and your greatest joy is me. Your joy was the whole point of my banging out the Big Bang. Do you think I had stars in my eyes instead of souls? Do you think I am more glorified by burning hydrogen than by burning hearts? By big acts of supernova explosions than by little acts of love?

"You don't understand your life because you are not simple. The meaning of life to you is me, and the meaning of life to me is you. The beloved is always at the center of the lover's vision. That's what love means. I waited billions of years for you, while the galaxies cooled, and those years were nothing to me because of my love. I was like Jacob waiting for Rachel: 'And Jacob served seven years for Rachel, and they seemed unto him but a few days, for the love he had to her.' (Genesis 29:20) *That* is why 'a thousand years are as yesterday' to me (Psalm 90:4): because I am love.

"Be like me. Be love. See all other things as relative to love, and as my love letters to you. See things as they are: all things in the universe and all things in your life are Jacob's ladders, highways for the commerce between two lovers, myself and yourself. If you see this, then you will see all your fearsome storms and all your Job-like pains as ice cream cones dropping. Better, you will see them as my cross. And since it is *my* cross, you will see it as a cross of love and life. Your very sufferings will be like the Mount of Transfiguration: through the prism of your faith in me and through the power of my wounds of love, your wounds will reflect my Sonlight and turn to gold and glory. I Jesus am your Midas touch."

We think we have believed the Good News that "God is love" (I John 4:8) and that He makes "all things work together for good for those who love Him" (Romans 8:28)—and we have, but our belief is mainly what Newman called "notional assent" rather than "real assent." It is assent to the truth of the idea more than to the reality. It is easy to say a total Yes to the truth of Christ. To do that is simply to be a Christian. But it is hard to say a total Yes to Christ. To do that is to be a saint.

Our faith is true, and precious, and priceless, but it is not *heavy* enough. It is like a beautiful golden cloud. When life deposits a heavy burden on us, it falls through the cloud like a cannonball because it is heavier than any cloud, even a golden one. Our faith must become more than a cloud; it must become a *thing*, a thing more real and solid and substantial than any burden. And that thing can only be "Jesus only." It cannot be "Jesus if" or "Jesus and" or "Jesus but." In Christ there are no ifs, ands, or buts. (II Corinthians 1:20)

2. The Overcoming of Legalism

No one defends legalism today, yet few escape it.

The only escape is truth, the truth about law. And that truth is that the purpose of law is to lead to Christ. ("The law was our schoolmaster to lead us to Christ."—Galatians 3:24.)

Law is good. (Romans 7:12) We need it for moral clarity, to define good and evil. This is true of both moral law and civil law. But while only criminals need worry about civil law, everyone has to worry about moral law. Only a few are civil law-breakers, but all are moral lawbreakers.

We worry about breaking many moral laws many times. For we know we are very creative at inventing new ways to sin and new excuses for repeating old sins. Christ is the single solution to all our sins. Sins are many and laws are many, but Christ is one.

Our inner moral lives seem complex. There are many laws, many temptations, many sins. Our external social life is also complex, increasingly so, sometimes crushingly so. That is why we hurry so: we are trying to do the impossible: everything. Perhaps there are a few people somewhere hiding in trees who are sane enough not to be affected by our worship of the clock, and who therefore still have and feel liberation and leisure and freedom in their lives—but I have never met them. Our worries and concerns are many, both spiritually and physically, both internally and externally. We are complex and worried externally only because we are complex and worried internally, just as there are external wars only because there are internal wars. (See James 4:1–3.) Simplicity would be liberation. But simplicity seems impossibly, unrealistically distant.

—Until we hear Christ's radical, liberating word that frees us from both physical and spiritual complexity and therefore from legalism; the liberating word He spoke to Martha. (Martha is us.) "Poor Martha. You are anxious and troubled about many things. But there is only one thing necessary." (Luke 10:42)

O Gospel! O news of a good beyond hope! O secret of success for both sanity and sanctity! O sweet substitute for psychiatry! Could it be true? What could this "one thing necessary" possibly be?

Christ does not tell us the answer, He *shows* us the answer: "Mary has chosen the better part." What did Mary choose? Jesus Himself. Jesus only. Mary forsook all else to sit at Jesus' feet. The "one thing necessary" is Jesus Himself. He is the one Messiah promised by all the laws and all the prophets, and He is promised to all of us and to all our needs.

Especially our moral needs. For the Christian, the moral life is simply Christ Himself living through the members of His Body, His Church, His people. Moral law only *describes* and *prescribes* that life; Christ *is* it, and *gives* it. He gives what He is. He gives Himself.

* * * * *

He gives it especially in the Eucharist. The Eucharist is His Body, and so is the Church. And just as the Eucharist is not a mere symbol or picture of Christ but Christ Himself, so the moral life of Christians, i.e. of Christ's Church, is not a mere picture but the real presence of Christ acting through His sinful, silly, stupid people.

The difference between His hidden presence in the Eucharist and His hidden presence in His people is that the Eucharist does not have two natures. It is perfect. It is 100% Christ and 0% bread and wine, while we are mixed and imperfect. We are 99% Adam and 1% Christ. Therefore we are not to worship His imperfect people, but we are to worship the Eucharist. What appears to be not-Christ in the Eucharist is Christ, but what appears to be not-Christ in fallen, sinful humanity really is not Christ. The Eucharistic bread is transubstantiated, while we are consubstantiated. The Lutheran theology of the Eucharist is right, but it's right about us, not about the Eucharist. ("Consubstantiation" means the belief that both Christ *and* bread and wine are really present in the Eucharist after the consecration.)

But though tiny and imperfect, Christ's presence in us is real. For being a Christian means real incorporation into Christ's real Body. And it's alive! It's a corpus, not a corpse. And that is the whole point of morality: Christ and His Body. Just as the whole point of houses is living, and the whole point of medicine is healing, and the whole point of science is knowing, so the whole point of religion is becoming little Christs, becoming Christ's Bride, becoming the Church, becoming His Body, becoming one with Him in body and spirit. (How many ways there are to say the same thing!) Christ makes morality into the farthest thing in the world from legalism: a romance, a marriage, a love affair with the Lord. How could we have thought of morality as dull and dehumanizing, repressive or confining? Only because we did not know its whole point: Him.

* * * * *

This second point (overcoming legalism) is the immediate consequence of the first point (personalism). Christian personalism means more than merely the idea that persons are important, even intrinsically valuable, and more than the idea that principles are for persons rather than persons for principles, and more than the idea that we should look at the personal subject who is doing the moral choosing and acting rather than merely at the object of that person's thinking, choosing, and acting. It means all of those things too, but you don't have to be a Christian to know all those principles. Christian personalism means above all that the ultimate object of the Christian's thinking, choosing, and acting is a Person: Christ. "Only one life; 'twill soon be past. Only what's done for Christ will last." My grandmother sewed those words into a sampler and put it on her dining room wall, and thus into the walls of my mind and heart. Thank you, Grandma. It has been over sixty years since I have seen that sampler, but I have not forgotten.

Jesus sums up the moral life in two words: "Follow Me." (John 1:43) All other great moral teachers—Moses, Buddha, Confucius, Lao Tzu, Socrates, Muhammad—said: "Follow my teaching." But Christ said: "Follow me." They said, "I teach the way," but Christ said "I *am* the way." Buddha said, "Look not to me, look to my *dharma* (doctrine)." Christ said, "Come unto me." (Matthew 11:28) Buddha said, "Be lamps unto yourselves." Christ said, "I am the light of the world." (John 8:12)

Philosophers seek wisdom. Christ *is* wisdom.

(I Corinthians 1:30) Therefore Christ is the fulfillment of philosophy.

Moralists seek righteousness. Christ *is* righteousness. (I Corinthians 1:30) Therefore Christ is the fulfillment of morality.

The difference between "follow my teaching" and "follow me" is like the difference between following a road map and following a car. Being a Christian is not worrying about getting all the details right in the map's directions; it's a high-speed car chase. "Follow *me!*"

And when the chase is over and we find Him, we find that He is "the hound of Heaven" who has been chasing us long before we began chasing Him. In fact, our very seeking Him was the result of His having sought us. In the words of the old hymn,

> I sought the Lord, and afterwards I knew
> He moved my soul to seek Him, seeking me.
> It was not I that found, O Savior true;
> No, I was found by Thee.

* * * * *

Christ is the single touchstone of morality. It is not possible to find an innocent act that does not welcome the name of Christ, or a sinful act that does. But He is more than the touchstone, He is also the goal, the good we seek, the "meaning of life," the *summum bonum,* the end, the "one thing necessary." Our hearts cannot be fooled about our ultimate good, even though our heads can. We know, and cannot not know, that nothing else is enough, that none of the other candidates for the office of king of our lives is really royal. Our hearts are restless until they rest in Him.

We have a "divine discontent," a "lover's quarrel with the world," a mysterious longing for a we-know-not-what. This longing feels like the heart-breakingly beautiful sound of a muffled bird's voice, so deep in our hearts that it is both infinitely far and infinitely close. It is like the Star of Bethlehem, a finger that moves restlessly through the sky and comes to rest only over the crib of the true Christ.

This is our supreme glory: the fact that our deepest longing is for divine glory, even though it seems ungraspable, unattainable, unimaginable, impossible, ineffable, indefinable, and infinite. This is also our supreme failure: that we long for a glory that is unattainable. Life is this *koan:* that the one thing we most want, we can least get; that on the one hand the glorious thing we want is nothing less than the glory of God and that on the other hand "All have fallen short of the glory of God." (Romans 3:23) The end—God—infinitely exceeds the means—all human effort.

And then we hear "the rest of the story," the Good News that God has done the impossible because "with God all things are possible" (Matthew 19:26); the Good News that God has let down from Heaven a ladder on which we could climb up to Him. (John 1:51; Genesis 28:12) We fell short of the glory of God, so the glory of God came down to us.

What is "the glory of God" that we have all fallen short of? It is Christ. Christ is the glory of God, the greatest glory of God. "In him all the fullness of God was pleased to dwell." (Colossians 1:19) The *Catechism of the Catholic Church* explicitly makes this simple equation: "The glory of God is Jesus Christ."

3. The Refutation of Relativism

The real presence of Christ in the moral life frees morality not only from legalism but also from relativism. The two are opposite errors: legalism sacrifices persons to principles, while relativism sacrifices principles for persons. But Christ is more absolute than any principle, and it is Christ, it is this personal absolute rather than impersonal legalism that is the refutation of moral relativism.

Moral relativism is the "politically correct" orthodoxy of our moldy culture. In the minds of the mind-molders, nothing is worse than "intolerance," and moral absolutism is intolerant. Thus the popularity of sayings like "Don't impose your values on me," "Different strokes for different folks," and "Live and let live."

No culture in history has ever embraced moral relativism and survived. Our own culture, therefore, will either (1) be the first, and disprove history's clearest lesson, or (2) persist in its relativism and die, or (3) repent of its relativism and live. There is no other option.

The greatest man in the worst century in history has called our culture a "culture of death." It is a culture that is increasingly sympathetic to "mercy killers" like "Doctor" Kevorkian because the culture itself is in the process of Kevorkianizing itself. It tolerates abortion because it is aborting itself. It therefore needs a far deeper therapy than good philosophical arguments refuting relativism. They are only an x-ray; we need a cure. The x-ray provides only the observation of the symptoms, the effects of the disease; we need a diagnosis of the disease that is causing the symptoms before we can prescribe for the cure. And the deepest diagnosis of the root cause of our culture's disease, in a single word, is Christlessness. Worse, it is Christophobia.

The strongest answer to moral relativism is not a perfect argument but a perfect person: Christ. For that is concrete evidence, real data, real presence. Meet Him, and relativism instantly shrivels like a vampire in the sunlight. The most irrefutable arguments are always facts, data, concrete reality. For instance, the most effective argument against abortion is simply to see one. That is why the most common operation in America is the only one never seen on any TV or movie screen.

The two things that convince people the most are facts and persons. Christ is both.

Our culture rejects Christian morality because it rejects Christ. It usually thinks of morality as helpful in other areas but as joyless and repressive in one area: sex. It does not know that morality is sexy: it is spiritual foreplay, spiritual courtship, spiritual marriage preparation on earth for our ecstatic consummation in eternity. It does not know that the point of morality is ultimately a marital union with God in Christ, which is an unending, unlimited, unimaginable ecstasy of self-giving, self-forgetful love. Does that sound like what our culture means by morality? Why not? Because it does not know Christ. That's why it thinks of morality as human rules, necessary but joyless, like baggage inspections at airports. It thinks that necessary goods are necessary evils! Its images of moral living are images of unfreedom: marching in lockstep in a parade, or coloring within the lines, or even the bars of a prison.

If it knew Christ, it would know that morality is more like sailing lessons for beginners, in little Sunfish in shallow waters. But those shallows are the same water, the same holy element, that we are destined to sail on forever, in great tall ships, wild and free, with the wind of the Holy Spirit in our sails and the Mind of God at the tiller. For our destiny is to sail the great deep of God Himself, and that is no longer impossible because God Himself has become a man and has come aboard our boat. To be a moral relativist when the Absolute Himself is beside you in the boat is as stupid as it is to be such a skeptic about truth that you cynically ask "What is truth?" to Truth Himself who is standing before you, and then authorize His murder.

4. The Secret of Moral Success

We know the good; we do not do it. C.S. Lewis says, rightly, that it is simply impossible to think clearly about life without admitting those two primary facts. (See the end of Part I of *Mere Christianity*.) We know the good because we can't *not* know it. God continues to enlighten our conscience. But we do not *do* it because we are not saints. The good that we would do, we do not, and the evil that we would not do, we do. (Romans 7:15) We are morally impotent. We have moral knowledge but not moral power.

The golden key of Christ's real presence unlocks this door too. Christ gives us not only the most profound understanding of morality but also the power to practice it. He does both in giving us Himself.

The very first words of the *Catechism of the Catholic Church*'s section on morality explains this: "Christian, recognize your dignity, and now that you share in God's own nature, do not return to your former condition by sinning. Remember who is your Head and of whose Body you are a member." The secret of moral success is simply to practice the presence of Christ, which is to "know thyself." Christ is not only our moral *authority* but our moral *identity*. We are not just members of His organization; we are members of His organism, His Body. "Members" means "organs"!

Look how literally St. Paul means that word ("members") in telling the Corinthian Christians what sexual immorality means now for a Christian: "Shall I take the members of Jesus Christ and make them (that is, make *Him*) members of a prostitute?" (I Corinthians 6:15)

Just as whatever we do to our brothers, we do to Christ, so what we do with ourselves we do with Christ. For we are His members just as much as they are.

Just thinking about His teachings and trying to practice them is like thinking about getting an A on a hard test and trying to answer all the questions right. But practicing His presence is like acknowledging Him sitting right beside you taking the test with you. His presence is to sin what light is to darkness, what the sun is to maggots, and what crucifixes are to vampires.

Nothing even remotely comparable to this exists in any secular morality. Christians and secularists agree that self-esteem is a cause of good moral behavior, since we act out our own perceived identities; but no secularist knows the greatest reason for self-esteem: the astonishing fact that by His grace we are not only His, but Him. (Remember II Peter 1:4.)

Moralists and philosophers can convince us that it's good to be good, but they can't make us good. Psychologists can take away our guilt feelings, but they can't take away our guilt.

Yet sinners do become saints. It happens. Some people do conquer moral impotence. Saints happen. And saints are always made from the same raw material: sinners. There is no other raw material. Look at St. Paul, St. Augustine, St. Francis, St. Ignatius: a persecuting bigot, a playboy sex addict, a rich fop, and a professional killer, and they all become great saints. How can this happen? What is the efficient cause of it? Ask them. They will all give you the same answer: the Golden Key, Jesus Christ.

* * * * *

Everybody knows that a saint is a great lover of God and man. And everybody knows that love is the greatest thing in the world. But not everybody knows what kind of love this is or where to get it. The answer to both questions is Christ.

First of all, love is defined by Christ. I

Corinthians 13, the most famous chapter in the Bible, the one about love, is a definition of Christ. But it is an actuality, not just a potentiality or ideal. The Gospels are a "show and tell" of Christ: for Christ not only tells us what love is but shows us what love is. The Cross is the "operative definition" of love. It is what happens when perfect love meets the fallen world. It was no accident.

Second, Christ is not only what love is, but Christ is also where you go to get it. To get crocodiles you must go to where crocodiles are. To get wet you must go to where water is. To get sunburnt, you must go out into the sunlight. And to get Sonburnt with His love, you must go out into the Sonlight. That's all. To those tired and thirsty for love He says simply: "Come unto me, all you who labor and are heavy laden, and I will give you rest." (Matthew 11:28) That is the simplest and most perfect formula for becoming a saint: go to Him.

The one and only thing that can ever save our world from disaster, from all the consequences of sin, is saints. And Jesus is the saint-maker. He was called "Jesus" ("Savior") not because He would save us only from the *punishment* that was due to our sins. The angel's command was: "You shall call his name 'Jesus' because he will save his people from their *sins*." (Matthew 1:21)

God will not rest until you are a saint. He demands it: "You must be perfect even as your Father in Heaven is perfect." (Matthew 5:48)

But we are not saints. Why?

The answer is very easy to find. Look into the mirror of your heart. Be utterly honest with yourself. Can you doubt that (to quote William Law) the only reason you are not a saint at this very moment is because you do not wholly want to be?

Oh, but I do want to be, you answer, quite honestly.

Yes, but not wholly.

What then can make our will whole? What is the secret of the saints? We have the same ideals, the same principles, the same beliefs, the same aspirations. Why do the saints live them so much better than we do? What is the secret of their success?

Paradoxically, we don't do enough good because we do too much good. That means two things: first, we are Marthas, worrying about many things, instead of Marys, simply loving "Jesus only." And second, we try to do it ourselves, asking God for "help," instead of realizing Step One of any Twelve-Step program, that we *can't* do it ourselves. Jesus has to do it. Our resources are tiny, His are unlimited.

A saint is a soldier who has burnt all his bridges behind him and sees "Jesus only" ahead of him.

That does not mean passivity any more than it means Martha-like activism. Giving yourself up to God is the least passive thing you can possibly do. It was that dynamo of activity, St. Paul, who said "I live, nevertheless not I, but Christ lives in me." (Galatians 2:20) It was another dynamo, John the Baptist, who said, "He must increase, but I must decrease." (John 3:30)

5. Jesus and Sex

When we hear the word "morality" today we automatically think of sexual morality. This is because we know that sex is by far the biggest moral battlefield in the world. Everyone speaks of the "sexual revolution." No one speaks of a corresponding moral revolution in any other area. In fact, the rest of the moral law is still pretty much in place in people's minds and hearts. No U.S. President would have survived revelations that he was a sadist, or a robber, or a murderer, or even a deliberate liar about anything else than sex.

Moral relativism is the new orthodoxy among our mind-molders in media and education. And almost all the justifications for the new moral relativism are sexual. No one wants a morality of "anything goes" or "different strokes for different folks" or "live and let live" or "don't be judgmental" when it comes to ecology, or economics, or penology, or terrorism, or even smoking. Only sex.

We do not justify murdering helpless innocents, except in the name of sex. If storks brought babies, there would be no abortions. Abortion is backup birth control, and birth control is the demand to have sex without having babies. The motor driving the abortion holocaust is sexual.

We do not justify any other practice whose clear results are (1) betraying your life's most intimate friend and your most solemn promise, (2) harming your children's happiness very deeply for the rest of their lives, and (3) destroying the most fundamental building block of human society. But we justify divorce, even though it has these three results, because it is in the name of sex. We are not allowed to steal another man's money without being put into jail, but we can steal another man's wife. You cannot betray your lawyer without being penalized, but you can betray your wife, and *she* is penalized. You cannot kill unborn bald eagles or blue whales without breaking the law, but you can kill your own unborn children without breaking the law.

Obviously, this society is not overstocked with philosophical wisdom or logical consistency. But there is little hope of restoring these commodities simply by arguments, however unanswerable they are. Try proving to a pothead that he needs to unscramble his brains. His brains are already scrambled, so the message will find no soil. Sex addicts will not think clearly any more than drug addicts will.

Yet, though thinking is not sufficient, it is necessary. Thinking unconfuses things. We must find the essence of our confusion and then find the golden key to the way out of that confusion.

The essence of the confusion is that we confuse sex with love. And Christ is the way out. Now watch how this works.

Here is the confusion: the Beatles sang: "All you need is love." But it isn't. Someone wrote a romantic novel with the title "Love Is Enough." But it isn't. Not the kind of love they mean. On the other hand, it *is* true that "all you need is love" and that "love is enough," for "God is love" and God is enough.

And here is the clearing-up of the confusion,

the apparent contradiction: What kind of love is God? The answer is Christ. Do you want to know what love ultimately is? Look there. Look at Christ. There is love. The definition is not abstract but as concrete as a crucifix.

No one in Western civilization can ignore the wisdom we received from Christ, that the greatest value is love. What we can and do ignore is how different that love is from all natural human loves, how challenging it is, how radical a change it requires. To explain it by an analogy, He called this change a "new birth," deliberately using as its image the single most radical change we have ever experienced in our natural lives. We confuse the love He was talking about (*agape*) either with sexual love (*eros*) or with subjective compassion and kindness, or with philanthropy, the objective deeds these feelings motivate us to perform. The confusion with sexual love is not rationally defensible, so it is unconscious; the confusion with inner feelings of compassion, or with external deeds of philanthropy, seems defensible, so it is usually conscious. But I Corinthians 13 explicitly refutes both.

Unlike all other forms of love, Christ's love is not easy, natural, or emotional; it is hard, supernatural, and an act of will, sometimes in the teeth of feelings. Was Mother Teresa's work of picking up the fly-infested, dying derelicts from the streets of Calcutta based on some sweet, cuddly *feeling* she had for them? Was she a necrophiliac? Did Jesus have the same *feelings* toward Judas that He had toward John? When His feelings changed, did His love change?

We do not usually ignore Christ's demand for love, but we do usually ignore how different that love is from all merely human loves. Differences are revealed by thought. We do not *think* about His saying "By this all men will know that you are my disciples: by the love you have for each other." (John 13:35) If that love had been a natural, generic, universal love already present in man, the saying would contradict itself. It would mean: "The world will see the difference between you and them by the fact that you all share the same kind of love." It meant, of course, exactly the opposite.

Now what difference does Christ and His love (*agape*) make to sex (*eros*)? What light does the Light of the World shed on the god of our world, sex, and on our Sexual Revolution?

Sex is the god of our world, our culture. It is our most non-negotiable demand. The teaching of Christ's faithful Church about sex is the main reason the world hates and fears the Church, for the Church is "judgmental" about our society's addiction and its real religion.

Christ revolutionizes the Sexual Revolution. How does He do that? Not by opposing religion to sex but by opposing real religion to false religion.

From Freud's point of view, religion is a substitute for sex; from Christ's point of view, sex is a substitute for religion. It's a pretty good substitute. Of all the things God created, it is one of the very best, and a natural icon of supernatural love and our supernatural destiny. Only very good things can be worshipped. You can't make a religion out of plumbing or insurance.

Let's explore how close sex is to religion. The center of religion, the ultimate end of religion, the "holy of holies" of religion, is spiritual marriage to God. The last event in human history, according to the Bible, at the end of the Apocalypse, is a wedding between the Lamb and His Bride, His Church. And the center of sex, and its greatest thrill, is the intimacy of intercourse, the almost-mystical overcoming of separateness and egotism, the identification with the other, in body and mind, the fact that the beloved allows you into his or her "holy of holies." This is a natural icon, image, shadow, prophecy, appetizer, and foretaste of that infinite and unimaginable ecstasy of Heaven that we were all made for. We are hard-wired for becoming one with God; that's why we are so thrilled at becoming one with each other. That's why self-forgetfulness, the transcendence of egotism, and the loss of control, in sexual orgasm is so mysteriously fulfilling. It's not just the purely physical sensation; it's the mystical meaning. The higher animals experience the same physical pleasure (watch dogs!), but they don't write mystical, romantic love poems about it, and they wouldn't write them even if they could write.

Animal sex is only a remote image of human romance, and human romance is a remote image of Heavenly ecstasy. The earthly intimacy with the beloved is a tiny, distant spark of the bonfire that is the Heavenly intimacy with God. Sex is a faint image of the Beatific Vision.

The Age of Faith invested its faith, its hope, and its love in that Heavenly ecstasy. Our Age of Apostasy has lost it, and therefore has become quite naturally attached to its image, human sex. The Sexual Revolution could not have happened without two causes, or conditions: (1) religious passion declined, and (2) the Pill enabled us to separate sex from procreation and lifelong responsibility.

Religion is not a pale substitute for sex but sex a pale substitute for real religion; because, as Aquinas says, "No man can live without joy; that is why a man deprived of spiritual joy goes over to carnal pleasures." (*ST* II-II, 35, 4 ad 2) The origin of the Sexual Revolution is religious. That's why its demands are so non-negotiable.

But when you have the real thing you are freed from addiction to its image. When you have a love (*agape*) relationship with God you are freed from addiction to love (*eros*) relationships to creatures. And only then, only when we do not so desperately need them, we can enjoy and appreciate creatures freely. The alcoholic is not free to appreciate alcohol, and the sexaholic is not free to appreciate sex.

What does Christ have to do with this? Everything. For Christ alone gives us intimacy with God. Therefore Christ alone is the answer to the Sexual Revolution.

To many people, this connection will seem bizarre. The question "What does Christ have to do with sex?" will sound suspiciously similar to the one the demons asked Christ when He was about to exorcise them from a man possessed: "What do you have to do with us, Jesus of Nazareth?" (Mark 1:24; Luke 4:34) How dare we bring these two things together? We must, because they are the two most passionate things in our lives.

Go over this again more deeply. Look at the deeper meaning of the Sexual Revolution. We live in a revolutionary time. More and deeper changes have happened in human history in the last half-millennium than in any other half-millennium, and more in the last century than in any other century. And the Sexual Revolution is surely the most radical revolution of our time. For "radical" means "about roots" (*radix*), and sex is the root of human life itself.

The most radical fruit of the Sexual Revolution is not in action but in thought. It is not what its enemies on the Right usually say it is, namely increased sexual immorality or promiscuity, even though the consequences of that are disastrous for the family and therefore for all society, especially for women. Nor is it what its friends on the Left usually say it is, namely increased knowledge and power by "sex education" and sexual experimentation and experience. Just the opposite: the most radical fruit of the Sexual Revolution is ignorance: ignorance of the most basic truth of all about sex, about its basic significance, that is, what it most basically means, or signifies, "what it's all about." Sex is about babies. Sex is the origin of new human life. That's *why* it's so ecstatic! Sex is for procreation, the closest approximation we can ever come to the divine ecstasy of creation. And that is what the Sexual Revolution forgets, denies, covers up, or forbids.

The most radical change of the Revolution was not in behavior. There have been all sorts of wild explosions of sexual behavior before in history, notably in dying Rome. The real revolution has been in thought. "All that we do is made from our thoughts," says Buddha, at the beginning of the *Dhammapada*. What Pope Paul VI prophetically called "the contraceptive *mentality*" was a more radical change than anyone foresaw, except Aldous Huxley in *Brave New World*. Contraception separates sex from babies. That is like separating food from nutrition, or eyes from seeing, or ice makers from ice, or churches from saints. (We do that too; how many of us see the Church first of all as a saint-making machine? But that's how St. Paul saw it. Remember that, and all the epistles light up.)

Both the Revolution's friends and its enemies usually say that the revolution consisted in the removal of restraint and censorship of sexual behavior. Its friends say this was good, and its enemies say it was not. But they are both wrong. Much more radical was the imposition of a new censorship, a censoring of the essence of sex, the meaning of sex. They were so fixated on the fact that *people* make sex that they forgot that sex makes people. They were so engrossed in psychology that they forgot biology.

The lies of the Revolution must be exposed. Divorce and abortion are two of them. The Revolution justifies divorce by an appeal to "compassion," but in fact divorce is terribly lacking in compassion to its innocent victims, children. It is like abortion that way. In fact it *is* an abortion: of the "one flesh" new person created by marriage. And that is the second lie: abortion, the primary sacrament of the Sexual Revolution and its most astonishing fruit.

Since the Sexual Revolution is based on a lie, it can be defeated only by telling the truth, the whole truth, and nothing but the truth about sex. This means not just No's but a Yes: dispelling fantasy by displaying reality, exposing the whole truth, the Big Picture. (That is what John Paul II did in his "theology of the body.")

The "big picture" includes two of the most basic truths of Christian theology, Creation and Incarnation. Christ believed the first, as a Jew, and He *was* the second.

Creation means that God loved into existence the whole material universe, including the human body and its sexuality. Christianity is the most materialistic religion in history. Matter is very good. God loves matter. Look how much of it He made!

Incarnation means God not only created matter but became matter! God became a material being! And He still is. He did not leave His human body behind when He ascended. The Ascension was not an undoing of the Incarnation. Christ took His human nature, human body and human soul, with Him to Heaven, where He has it forever.

The doctrine of Creation means that all matter is holy because God made it, but the doctrine of the Incarnation means the human body is most holy because God took it into His own being, married it, in an indissoluble union. (What God has joined together, no man can put asunder.) Christ became incarnate to redeem us, and redemption was physical. It did not happen just by teaching or good example. It happened by Christ physically giving us His blood, on the Cross, not just mentally being willing to do this. Tertullian said, "the flesh is the hinge of salvation." "No other blood will do."

Creation (of matter), Incarnation (into human matter), Ascension (of His material human body), Eucharist, "new heavens *and new earth*"—God cherishes matter like an artist. Only such a religion could have produced John Paul's "theology of the body." It will be his trademark forever, as the "restless heart" is St. Augustine's and as holy poverty is St. Francis's, and as the marriage of faith and reason is St. Thomas's.

The theology of the body is totally Christocentric. Christ does not *teach* the theology of the body; Christ *is* the theology of the body.

At the heart of the theology of the body is the vision of sex as an icon of the Trinity and of our final, mystical Heavenly destiny to be married to God. God is not just an individual; God is a family, a Trinity, a family of Father, Son, and Spirit. Thus the family is Godlike because God is a family.

God is a Trinity because He is love, complete love, therefore Lover, Beloved, and Loving. He is not just a lov*er*, but "God is *love*." (I John 4:8) And that is why human love, especially human sexual love, is Godlike: because God is love.

This is Christocentric because Christ alone

reveals the Trinity. (Only Christians believe it.) Christ is our fundamental data for the doctrine of the Trinity. Christ is the reason we know that God is not just one lonely person but Father, Son, and Spirit: Christ called His Father God, and He called Himself God, and He called the Spirit They would send God; and yet as a Jew He knew there is only one God. Therefore God *is* Father and Son and Holy Spirit.

And the Trinity is the ultimate meaning of sex. For we are made in God's image, and that means sex. The very first time scripture uses the phrase "the image of God" (Genesis 1:27), it identifies it as "male and female."

How important is the theology of the body? That depends on how important the Sexual Revolution is. The importance of St. George depends on the importance of the dragon. The importance of Dr. Van Helsing depends on the importance of Dracula.

And how important is the Sexual Revolution? That depends on how important the family is—for exactly the same reason.

And how important is the family? It is only the basis for all human society, in fact for human existence.

Four of the most stable, successful, internally peaceful, and long-lived societies in history were the Jewish (Mosaic), the Confucian, the Islamic, and the Roman. They lasted, respectively, about 35, 21, 14, and 7 centuries, for one overriding reason: because they all greatly respected the family.

I think the family is even more important to God than doctrinal orthodoxy, because the family is about the very image of God in man. Islam and Mormonism are theological heresies, but God is blessing them and they are expanding faster than Christianity today because Muslims and Mormons are much more faithful than Christians to the family, marriage, sexual morality, and procreation. They are resisting the Sexual Revolution. We are succumbing to it.

This is outrageous, because the definitive answer to the Sexual Revolution is not Muhammad or Joseph Smith but Jesus, who not only reveals but incarnates the mystery of the holiness of sex, marriage, and the family as a sacred sign of our ultimate destiny, spiritual marriage to God. Jesus does not just tell us the Big Picture; He *is* the Big Picture. He does not just teach us the Word of God about sex. He *is* the Word of God about sex. He does not merely reveal the spiritual marriage;

He *is* the spiritual marriage. In Christ we have more than the Big Picture; we have the Big Person.

6. Christ and Social Ethics: Solidarity

The fundamental problem of society is *glue*. What glues naturally selfish individuals together? We are naturally selfish. That is the empirically verifiable formulation of the doctrine of Original Sin. Selfishness divides, community unites. What melds selfishness into community? Is it force? Or is it social justice?

Neither. It is solidarity. Solidarity (*Sobornost* in Russian, *Solidarinosc* in Polish) has always been more powerful than justice as human glue, for justice is abstract and rational, while solidarity is concrete and mystical.

But what is the basis of solidarity? It is not merely our common origin, in Adam, but our common end, in Christ.

Secularists say our common origin is apes and our common end is death. Not a very good basis for solidarity!

The world rightly praises (when it is sane) and practices (when it is moral) respect for all human lives, including the smallest and weakest and neediest and most vulnerable, the most "useless." But

short"? Not just by social contracts and technologies. Hitler's Germany, Stalin's Russia, and Mao's China had both, and life was still solitary, poor, nasty, brutish, and short.

Again, Christ does not merely teach the answer, Christ is the answer. He does not point us to our peace; He is our peace.

7. Jesus and Politics: Is He Right or Left?

All political issues today are seen through the prism of Right vs. Left, the political "us vs. them." The categories are all-encompassing thought-savers, knee-jerks that allow us to avoid thinking about each issue on its own merits. But the categories, and the polarization they create, is even more indefensible when applied to Christ because it means judging Christ by the fallen world rather than vice versa.

The polarization is also harmful to morality because it lets us be selectively moral, selectively idealistic—which means selectively immoral and pragmatic. If we take the high road on abortion, euthanasia, and sexuality, we can take the low road on war, poverty, and pollution; or vice versa. Even when we focus on a specific question like whether all human lives are intrinsically valuable, these categories allow us the moral schizophrenia to say yes when we address abortion and no to that same question when we address war and capital punishment—or vice versa. It's not just that we give wrong answers (I'm not sure what the right answers are in particular about a particular war or capital punishment in a particular case), it's that we have self-contradictory principles.

Only from the viewpoint of the straight can we judge the skewered. Christ is the straight, the plumb line—both when He is explicitly known, by divine revelation, and when He is implicitly known, by conscience and the natural law. He brings to all issues God's natural order to judge man's unnatural disorders. Therefore, He does that to politics too.

He also unites the proper concerns of Right and Left, for He is the straight path ("I am the Way") from which both Right and Left turns depart. He gives a stronger reason for the rightful concerns of both Right and Left than either Right or Left can do.

For instance, why feed the poor? Because the poor are Christ in disguise. Not just because of political correctness or individual sentiment.

Why love sinners, as the Left does, and why

hate sins, as the Right does? Why love addicts to drugs, violence, money, or sex? And why hate their addictions? For the same reason. Because Christ does. That's why we should be more compassionate to sinners than liberals are and more uncompassionate to sins than conservatives are. For the same reason: Christ.

Why insist on doctrinal orthodoxy? Not just out of correctness but out of loyalty to Christ. Why speak of sin and salvation, two words that scandalize the secularist? Not just to refute secularism but because of Christ. Christ not only spoke of sin and salvation, Christ *is* salvation.

Why preach and practice the "social gospel"? Not to be politically correct, or to refute the Fundamentalists, but because Christ did.

Why be universalistic and inclusive and ecumenical? Not to sneer at xenophobia, isolationism, and provincialism, but because Christ was and is universalistic. Christ is not a local tribal deity.

Why insist on "the scandal of particularity," and on the concrete, visible, particular, and exclusive claims of Christ to be the one and only Savior? Not to stick it to the liberals, but because Christ is particular and concrete and visible and exclusive and literal.

Why be progressive and radical and creative and in love with the new? Why be open to the winds like a sail? Because Christ is.

Why be faithful and stick-in-the-mud traditionalist, like an anchor? Because Christ is "the same yesterday, today, and forever."

Why be a "bleeding heart liberal"? Because Christ is. Why be a "hard-headed conservative"? Because Christ is.

Many have substituted Liberalism or Conservatism or some other ism for Christ, and coopted Christ for their cause. Christ cannot be coopted for any cause; all causes must be coopted for Him. All isms are abstractions. Even the perfect ism, if there is one, cannot save us and cannot love us.

The special danger of the religious Right is to worship Christ's doctrines instead of Christ, confusing the sign with the thing signified. The Right is absolutely right to insist on being right and to insist on absolutes. But a finger is for pointing at the moon; woe to the fool who mistakes the finger for the moon.

The special danger of the religious Left is to worship Christ's values instead of Christ. That is just as abstract as the Right's substituting Christ's doctrines for Christ. They are also only pointing fingers.

The Right argues that the Left is vague, but even the true and precise doctrines of the Right are vague compared with Christ. Everything is. The Left argues that the Right is hard, but even the soft, compassionate heart of a liberal is hard compared with Christ. Everything is.

Right and Left cannot convince and convert each other for the same reason that the Pharisees and the Sadducees could not convince and convert each other. For what a Pharisee needs is not a little softening of the head, a little dose of worldliness, pop psychology, relativism, and subjectivism. What he needs is Christ. And what a Sadducee needs is not a little hardening of the heart, a little arrogance, a little bit of Scrooge or Machiavelli or Darwinian "survival of the fittest." What he needs is Christ.

And our society needs nothing less, split as it is between Left and Right today just as Jesus' society was split between Sadducees and Pharisees in His time.

Earthly societies are not eternal, as souls are. Yet Christ is the Savior of societies as well as souls. Our society is dying because it has turned the holy name of its Savior into a curse word. Christophobia is the poison that is killing our society. Our secularists are making us forget Christ faster than we are making them remember Him: that is why our society is dying. Its blood supply is drying up. The Precious Blood is evaporating. We are losing more blood each day.

The answer is scandalously simple, unless Christ and Christianity and the Bible and the Church and Christ's apostles and all the saints are liars. The answer is that there is only one hope, for societies as well as souls: "What must I do to be saved?" "Believe on the Lord Jesus Christ and you shall be saved." (Acts 11:14)

Is that too simple and childish for you? Are you too "advanced" and "adult" for that? Remember what "advanced" tooth decay looks like. Remember what our society means by "adult." Remember what "adult" movies mean. And then put that against *The Passion of the Christ*. And then "choose ye this day whom ye will serve." (Joshua 24:15)

Conclusion

YOU DIDN'T EXPECT A book on philosophy to end like that, did you? But that's the way the world's greatest philosopher ended His philosophy. The last words of Christ in the Bible, through His prophet John, in the Apocalypse, say the same thing. (Read Revelation 22.) For this is the most important thing anyone can ever say, the most momentous choice we can make, the choice between everything and nothing, being and non-being, light and darkness, Heaven and Hell, Christ and Antichrist—and if philosophy has nothing to say about that, then the hell with it.

Index

Scripture Quotations